Teach For All Counter-Narratives

This book is part of the Peter Lang Education list.
Every volume is peer reviewed and meets
the highest quality standards for content and production.

PETER LANG
New York • Bern • Berlin
Brussels • Vienna • Oxford • Warsaw

Teach For All Counter-Narratives

International Perspectives on a Global Reform Movement

Edited by T. Jameson Brewer,
Kathleen deMarrais, & Kelly L. McFaden

PETER LANG
New York • Bern • Berlin
Brussels • Vienna • Oxford • Warsaw

Library of Congress Cataloging-in-Publication Data

Names: Brewer, T. Jameson, editor. | DeMarrais, Kathleen Bennett, editor. |
   McFaden, Kelly L., editor.
Title: Teach for All counter-narratives: international perspectives on a
   global reform / edited by T. Jameson Brewer, Kathleen deMarrais, and
   Kelly L. McFaden.
Description: New York: Peter Lang, 2020.
   Includes bibliographical references and index.
Identifiers: LCCN 2019032395 | ISBN 978-1-4331-7212-0 (hardback: alk. paper)
ISBN 978-1-4331-7211-3 (paperback: alk. paper) | ISBN 978-1-4331-5716-5 (ebook pdf)
   ISBN 978-1-4331-5717-2 (epub) | ISBN 978-1-4331-5718-9 (mobi)
Subjects: LCSH: Educational equalization—Case studies. | Educational
   Change—Case studies. | People with social disabilities—Education—Case
   studies. | Teach for All (Project)—Case studies.
Classification: LCC LC213 .T43 | DDC 379.2/6—dc23
LC record available at https://lccn.loc.gov/2019032395
DOI 10.3726/b14043

Bibliographic information published by **Die Deutsche Nationalbibliothek**.
Die Deutsche Nationalbibliothek lists this publication in the "Deutsche
Nationalbibliografie"; detailed bibliographic data are available
on the Internet at http://dnb.d-nb.de/.

The paper in this book meets the guidelines for permanence and durability
of the Committee on Production Guidelines for Book Longevity
of the Council of Library Resources.

© 2020 Peter Lang Publishing, Inc., New York
29 Broadway, 18th floor, New York, NY 10006
www.peterlang.com

All rights reserved.
Reprint or reproduction, even partially, in all forms such as microfilm,
xerography, microfiche, microcard, and offset strictly prohibited.

Printed in the United States of America

TJB: *for Abigail & Addison, who broadened my view of the world.*

KD: *for Jennifer Walker Marin, a wonderful teacher and scholar.*

KLM: *for Luna, whose insistence on living in the moment makes everything seem manageable.*

Table of Contents

List of Illustrations ix

Introduction 1
    T. JAMESON BREWER, KATHLEEN DEMARRAIS, AND KELLY L. MCFADEN

Section I: Colonialism, Social Justice, Inequality, and Deficit Ideologies

1. *The Non-Project* 13
    JENNY ELLIOTT

2. *A Tale from the Tail of the Fish* 25
    NICKIE MUIR

3. *Disparities Between Expectations and Impact in Fellows' Experience of an Alternative Teaching Program in China* 39
    YUE MELODY YIN AND HILARY HUGHES

4. *Teach First Ask Questions Later: Experiencing a Policy Entrepreneur in New Zealand* 55
    SAM OLDHAM

Section II: Leadership Cultivation Over Teaching

5. *Leaders in the Community or Educators in the Classroom? Problematic Dual Roles of Fellows at Teach For China* 69
    SARA G. LAM, TONGJI PHILIP QIAN AND FAN ADA WANG

6. *Teach For All in Latvia: A Case Study and Warning to the World* 83
    ELĪNA BOGUSA AND IEVA BĒRZIŅA

7. Meritocracy and Leadership: The Keys to Social and Educational Change According to Enseñá por Argentina   93
    VICTORIA MATOZO AND ADRIANA SAAVEDRA

8. "We aren't teachers, we are leaders": Situating the Teach For India Programme   113
    VIDYA K. SUBRAMANIAN

9. Sign of the Times: Teach For Sweden and the Broken Swedish Education System   135
    P.S. MYERS

Index   149

Illustrations

Figure I.1. TFA & TFAll global locations. 4
Table I.1. Key issues in chapters. 5
Table 3.1. The demographic characteristics of interview participants. 44

Introduction

T. JAMESON BREWER, KATHLEEN DEMARRAIS, AND KELLY L. MCFADEN

Teach For All: Exporting Solutions in Search of Problems

The international spin-off organization of the USA-domestic organization of Teach For America (TFA), Teach For All (TFAll) represents the logical progression of pro-privatization and pro-marketization reforms that have swept the globe in the years following the widespread growth of neoliberalism that began in the mid 1980s (Apple, 2012; Ball, 1994, 2003, 2007, 2012; Brewer & Myers, 2015; Elmore, 2013; Giroux, 2004; Harvey, 2005; Peters, 2011; Weiner, 2011) and have dramatically reimagined teacher preparation and the role of educators (Brewer & Cody, 2014; Brewer & deMarrais, 2015; Gorlewski & Gorlewski, 2013; Lubienski & Brewer, 2019). As such, TFAll and a book sharing the stories of those who have been impacted by the organization find deep roots in the development and growth of its parent organization TFA that began in 1990 and has spread rapidly across the globe over the past decade. Below we explore the implications of this growth across the globe to provide a contextual backdrop through which to understand the chapters that follow.

We released *Teach For America Counter-Narratives: Alumni Speak Up and Speak Out* in 2015 and the book was met with what was, honestly, more interest among researchers, the general public, and popular media than we imagined. Esther Cepeda, a nationally-syndicated columnist, suggested in a national column in all of the major newspapers in the country that *Teach For America Counter-Narratives: Alumni Speak Up and Speak Out* was "explosive and jaw-dropping" and that the book served as "a cautionary tale to those studying the education reform movement" (Ravitch, 2015) and "eviscerated the myth of TFA's unmitigated success" (Schaefer, 2015). Following popular-press stories citing the book at NPR (Donnella, 2015; Rhodes, 2015), *The Daily Beast* (Allen, 2015), *Jacobin* (Jacobin, 2015), *AlterNet* (Millen, 2015), *The Chronicle of Philanthropy* (The Chronicle of Philanthropy, 2015),

The Washington Post (Brewer, 2015; Chovnick, 2015), *NonProfit Quarterly* (Levine & McCambridge, 2015), and The Bookings Institution (Hansen, 2015), TFA recruitment numbers began to drop precipitously and the organization began laying off staff members (Brown, 2016; Scott, 2016)—a result that some attributed directly to our book (Teran, 2016). We remain honored to have been in a position to share the stories of TFA corps members and alumni in a way that had never been done before. We are equally as proud to now expand that platform on an international scale.

Our collection of narratives on TFA was the first of its kind in that it gave voice to dissenters who had largely felt pressured by TFA to remain silent and, in some cases, forced to remain silent by TFA's multi-million dollar public relations campaigns to marginalize critical voices (Joseph, 2014). That collection of TFA alumni narratives highlighted twenty perspectives of TFA spanning the entirety of the organization's history and explored the ways in which TFA engaged in recruiting and training, approached issues related to diversity and race, and responded to critique and criticism. Our first book four years ago came about from emails sent to Jameson from TFA corps members and alumni who were seeking an outlet to share their stories. This international follow-up also arose from emails and conversations following the release of the USA-domestic counter-narratives book on the need for a collection of international perspectives surrounding TFAll.

About Teach For All (TFAll)

At the time of the release of *Teach For America Counter-Narratives: Alumni Speak Up and Speak Out* there was, and continues to be, a growing body of academic literature surrounding TFA (Anderson, 2013a, 2013b; Brewer, 2013, 2014; Brewer, Kretchmar, Sondel, Ishmael, & Manfra, 2016; Brewer & Wallis, 2015; Carter, Amrein-Beardsley, & Hansen, 2011; Cersonsky, 2012; Cody, 2012; Crawford-Garrett, 2013; Darling-Hammond, Holtzman, Gatlin, & Vasquez Heilig, 2005; deMarrais, Lewis, & Wenner, 2013; Donaldson & Johnson, 2011; Hartman, 2011; Kovacs, 2011; Kovacs & Slate-Young, 2013; Kretchmar, Sondel, & Ferrare, 2014; La Londe, Brewer, & Lubienski, 2015; Labaree, 2010; Lahann & Reagan, 2011; Maier, 2012; Miner, 2010; Redding & Smith, 2016; Scott, Trujillo, & Rivera, 2016; Stephens, 2011; Trujillo & Scott, 2014; Vasquez Heilig & Jez, 2010; Veltri, 2010, 2012). However, there were nearly no accounts or narratives outside of the academic body of literature from the words of TFA corps members and alumni. Similarly, while there is a smaller, but growing, body of academic literature that has sought to explore and understand TFAll both within specific cultural and country contexts as well as a global phenomenon (Friedrich, Walter, &

Colmenares, 2015; La Londe et al., 2015; Straubhaar & Friedrich, 2015) but often does not include narratives from those on-the-ground. TFAll is, at the time of this writing, celebrating its 10th anniversary as it currently operates in 48 countries across the globe (Teach For All, n.d.) and continues to expand (see Figure I.1).

Operating from an assumption that schools have failed and traditionally certified teachers are to blame, TFA and TFAll operationalize Wendy Kopp's vision that teaching is not a profession but rather a temporary role for those with prestigious backgrounds to fill (Kopp, 1989, 1991, 2001, 2013; Kopp & Farr, 2011; Kopp & Roekel, 2011). Involvement in TFAll organizations carries with it the same façade of "manufactured expertise" (Brewer, 2016) as it does in TFA as alumni of TFAll move quickly into policymaking positions to further promote agendas favorable to TFAll and the Global Education Reform Movement or GERM (Sahlberg, 2012).

About This Book

In *Teach For America Counter-Narratives: Alumni Speak Up and Speak Out* we noted the importance that narratives and counter-narratives play by pointing out that,

> Narratives, storytelling, and counter-stories can be transformative and empowering for educators, students, and community members. These methods can make public what many already know but have not spoken out loud: There are futures and lives at stake in the process we call *education*. (Fernández, 2002, p. 60) [Emphasis in the original]

We believe that Fernández's words remain applicable to this collection of international counter-narratives. We sought to curate a diverse collection of narratives from across the TFAll network in an effort to provide as much of a diverse perspective as possible (see Table I.1). In the chapters that follow you will read narratives from India, Sweden, the United Kingdom, South Africa, New Zealand, China, Argentina, and Latvia. While each region/country offers its own unique cultural perspective on TFAll, the chapters that follow explicate consistent themes that emerge regardless of the context. Overall, like their TFA counterparts, iterations of TFAll across the globe consistently ignore cultural and contextual factors in their delivery of pedagogy. Additionally, across the majority of contexts, TFAll organizations value the work of alumni impacting policy decisions or moving into leadership positions more than they value the actual work of teaching as TFAll organizations continue working to leverage a myriad of pro-privatization and standardization reforms throughout the globe.

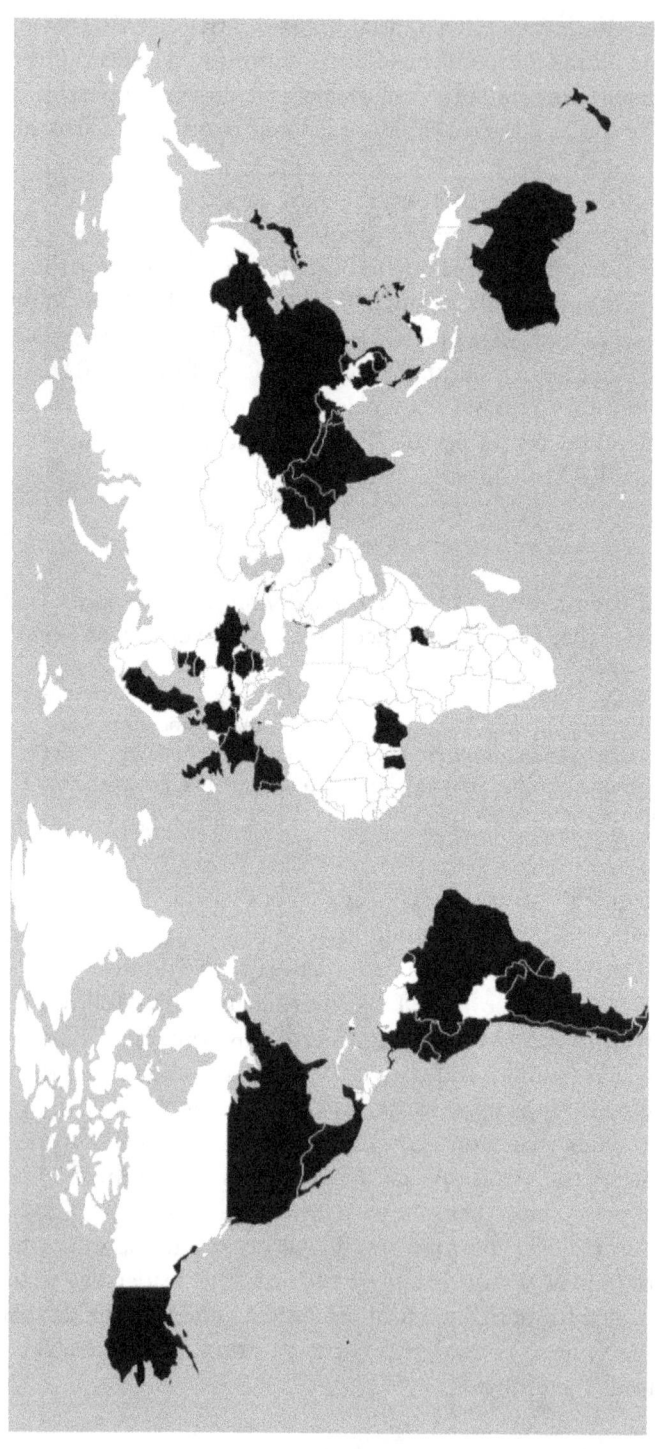

Figure I.1. TFA & TFAll global locations.

Table I.1. Key issues in chapters.

Author	TFAll Location	Key Concepts
Colonialism, Social Justice, Inequality, and Deficit Ideologies		
1. Jenny Elliott	United Kingdom and South Africa	• Colonialism • Bait and switch • Hidden Agendas
2. Nickie Muir	New Zealand	• Faux elitism and faux activism • Corporate sponsorship versus social justice
3. Yue Melody Yin & Hilary Hughes	China	• Expectations versus Reality • Deficit Ideologies • Cultural and contextual importance
4. Sam Oldham	New Zealand	• TFAll spin versus reality • Savior-mentality • TFAll contributes to inequality
Leadership Cultivation Over Teaching		
5. Sara G. Lam, Tongji Philip Qian & Fan Ada Wang	China	• Rural Education • Resistance • Teaching versus Leadership Cultivation
6. Elīna Bogusa & Ieva Bērzina	Latvia	• Alumni pipeline into policymaking • Case study of expansive TFAll political control
7. Victoria Matozo & Adriana Saavedra	Argentina	• Inconsistencies between TFAll ideology and the realities of teaching • Financial struggles
8. Vidya K. Subramanian	India	• Corporate influences • Leadership elevated over teaching
9. P.S. Myers	Sweden	• Leadership elevated over teaching • Markets versus democracy

References

Allen, S. (2015). Is Teach For America flunking out? Retrieved from https://www.thedailybeast.com/is-teach-for-america-flunking-out

Anderson, A. (2013a). Teach For America and symbolic violence: A Bourdieuian analysis of education's next quick-fix. *Urban Review*, 46(1).

Anderson, A. (2013b). Teach For America and the dangers of deficit thinking. *Critical Education*, 4(11), 1–20.

Apple, M. (2012). Afterword on neoliberalism, the current crisis, and the politics of hope. In M. Lall (Ed.), *Policy, discourse and rhetoric: How new labour challenged social justice democracy* (pp. 141–150). Rotterdam, Netherlands: Sense Publishers.

Ball, S. (1994). *Education reform: A critical and post-structural approach*. Bristol, PA: Open University Press.

Ball, S. (2003). *Class strategies and the education market: The middle classes and social advantage.* New York, NY: RoutledgeFalmer.

Ball, S. (2007). *Education plc: Understanding private sector participation in public sector education.* New York, NY: Routledge.

Ball, S. (2012). *Global education inc.: New policy networks and the neo-liberal imaginary.* New York, NY: Routledge.

Brewer, T. J. (2013). From the trenches: A Teach For America corps member's perspective. *Critical Education, 4*(12), 1–17.

Brewer, T. J. (2014). Accelerated burnout: How Teach For America's academic impact model and theoretical framework can foster disillusionment among its corps members. *Educational Studies, 50*(3), 246–263.

Brewer, T. J. (2015). Teach For America's biggest problem isn't green teachers or failing schools: It's that it can't take criticism. Retrieved from https://www.washingtonpost.com/posteverything/wp/2015/10/20/teach-for-americas-biggest-problem-isnt-green-teachers-or-failing-schools-its-that-it-cant-take-criticism/

Brewer, T. J. (2016). *Purposeful and lasting effects: An examination of teach for America's impact on the teaching profession, hiring practices, and educational leadership.* (Ph.D.), University of Illinois at Urbana-Champaign.

Brewer, T. J., & Cody, A. (2014). Teach For America: The neoliberal alternative to teacher professionalism. In J. A. Gorlewski, B. Porfilio, D. A. Gorlewski, & J. Hopkins (Eds.), *Effective or wise? Teaching and the meaning of professional dispositions in education* (pp. 77–94). New York, NY: Peter Lang.

Brewer, T. J., & deMarrais, K. (Eds.). (2015). *Teach For America counter-narratives: Alumni speak up and speak out.* New York, NY: Peter Lang.

Brewer, T. J., Kretchmar, K., Sondel, B., Ishmael, S., & Manfra, M. (2016). Teach For America's preferential treatment: School district contracts, hiring decisions, and employment practices. *Educational Evaluation and Policy Analysis, 24*(15), 1–38.

Brewer, T. J., & Myers, P. S. (2015). How neoliberalism subverts equality and perpetuates poverty in our nation's schools. In S. N. Haymes, M. V. d. Haymes, & R. Miller (Eds.), *The Routledge handbook of poverty in the United States* (pp. 190–198). New York, NY: Routledge.

Brewer, T. J., & Wallis, M. (2015). #TFA: The intersection of social media and education reform. *Critical Education, 6*(14), 1–18.

Brown, E. (2016). Teach For America applications fall again, diving 35 percent in three years. Retrieved from https://www.washingtonpost.com/news/education/wp/2016/04/12/teach-for-america-applications-fall-again-diving-35-percent-in-three-years/?utm_term=.0b4e7ae60fe8

Carter, H., Amrein-Beardsley, A., & Hansen, C. (2011). So not amazing! Teach For America corps members' evaluation of the first semester of their teacher preparation program. *Teachers College Record, 113*(5), 861–894.

Cersonsky, J. (2012). Teach For America's deep bench. Retrieved from http://prospect.org/article/teach-america%E2%80%99s-deep-bench

Chovnick, W. (2015). Good intentions gone bad: Teach For America's transformation from a small, humble non-profit into an elitist corporate behemoth. In T. J. Brewer & K. deMarrais (Eds.), *Teach For America counter-narratives: Alumni speak up and speak out*. New York, NY: Peter Lang.

Cody, A. (2012). TFA says 8 year claim is an estimate, "not really appropriate for publicizing". Retrieved from http://blogs.edweek.org/teachers/living-in-dialogue/2012/12/tfa_says_8_year_claim_is_an_es.html

Crawford-Garrett, K. (2013). *Teach For America and the struggle for urban school reform*. New York, NY: Peter Lang.

Darling-Hammond, L., Holtzman, D. J., Gatlin, S. J., & Vasquez Heilig, J. (2005). Does teacher preparation matter? Evidence about teacher certification, Teach For America, and teacher effectiveness. *Education Policy Analysis Archives*, *13*(42), 1–51.

deMarrais, K., Lewis, J., & Wenner, J. (2013). Bringing Teach For America into the forefront of teacher education: Philanthropy meets spin. *Critical Education*, *4*(11), 1–26.

Donaldson, M., & Johnson, S. (2011). TFA teachers: How long do they teach? Why do they leave. Retrieved from http://www.edweek.org/ew/articles/2011/10/04/kappan_donaldson.html

Donnella, L. (2015). 2 Teach For America alums say TFA has big problems when it comes to race. Retrieved from https://www.npr.org/sections/codeswitch/2015/10/14/447217749/two-teach-for-america-alums-say-the-program-has-big-problems-when-it-comes-to-ra

Elmore, J. M. (2013). Neoliberalism and teacher preparation: Systematic barriers to critical democratic education. In P. L. Thomas (Ed.), *Becoming and being a teacher: Confronting traditional norms to create new democratic realities* (pp. 107–118). New York, NY: Peter Lang.

Fernández, L. (2002). Telling stories about school: Using critical race and Latino critical theories to document Latina/Latino education and resistance. *Qualitative Inquiry*, *8*(45), 45–65.

Friedrich, D., Walter, M., & Colmenares, E. (2015). Making all children count: Teach for all and the universalizing appeal of data. *Educational Policy Analysis Archives*, *23*(48), 1–21.

Giroux, H. A. (2004). *The terror of neoliberalism: Authoritarianism and the eclipse of democracy*. Aurora, Ontario: Garamond Press.

Gorlewski, J. A., & Gorlewski, D. A. (2013). Too late for public education? Becoming a teacher in a neoliberal era. In P. L. Thomas (Ed.), *Becoming and being a teacher: Confronting traditional norms to create new democratic realities* (pp. 119–134). New York, NY: Peter Lang.

Hansen, M. (2015). Losing its luster? New evidence on teach for America's impact on student learning. Retrieved from https://www.brookings.edu/blog/brown-center-chalkboard/2015/10/27/losing-its-luster-new-evidence-on-teach-for-americas-impact-on-student-learning/

Hartman, A. (2011). Teach For America: The hidden curriculum of liberal do-gooders. *Jacobin*. Retrieved from https://www.jacobinmag.com/2011/12/teach-for-america

Harvey, D. (2005). *A brief history of neoliberalism*. Oxford: Oxford University Press.

Jacobin. (2015). Taking on TFA. Retrieved from https://www.jacobinmag.com/2015/10/tfa-wendy-kopp-corporate-education-reform-new-orleans/

Joseph, G. (2014). This is what happens when you criticize Teach For America: An internal memo reveals how TFA's obsessive PR game covers up its lack of results in order to justify greater expansion. Retrieved from http://www.thenation.com/article/186481/what-happens-when-you-criticize-teach-america#

Kopp, W. (1989). *An argument and plan for the creation of the teacher corps*. (Bachelors), Princeton, St. Louis, MO.

Kopp, W. (1991). Replace certification with recruitment. Retrieved from http://www.edweek.org/ew/articles/1991/10/09/06kopp.h11.html

Kopp, W. (2001). *One day, all children: The unlikely triumph of Teach For America and what I learned along the way*. Cambridge, MA: PublicAffairs, Perseus Books Group.

Kopp, W. (2013). 3 myths about changing the world. Retrieved from http://www.huffingtonpost.com/wendy-kopp/3-myths-about-changing-th_b_3304015.html

Kopp, W., & Farr, S. (2011). *A chance to make history: What works and what doesn't in providing an excellent education for all*. New York, NY: PublicAffairs, Perseus Books Group.

Kopp, W., & Roekel, D. V. (2011). Column: 3 ways to improve the USA's teachers. Retrieved from http://usatoday30.usatoday.com/news/opinion/forum/story/2011-12-20/teachers-education-public-schools/52121868/1

Kovacs, P. (2011). Philip Kovacs: Huntsville takes a closer look at Teach For America's "research". Retrieved from http://blogs.edweek.org/teachers/living-in-dialogue/2011/12/huntsvilles_research-based_com.html

Kovacs, P., & Slate-Young, E. (2013). An analysis of Teach For America's research page. *Critical Education*, 4(11), 67–80.

Kretchmar, K., Sondel, B., & Ferrare, J. (2014). Mapping the terrain: Teach For America, charter school reform, and corporate sponsorship. *Journal of Education Policy*, 29(6), 742–759.

La Londe, P., Brewer, T. J., & Lubienski, C. (2015). Teach For America and Teach For All: Creating an intermediary organization network for global education reform. *Education Policy Analysis Archives*, 23(47), 1–28.

Labaree, D. (2010). Teach For America and teacher ed: Heads they win, tails we lose. *Journal of Teacher Education*, 61(1–2), 48–55.

Lahann, R., & Reagan, E. M. (2011). Teach For America and the politics of progressive neoliberalism. *Teacher Education Quarterly*, 38(1), 7–27.

Levine, M., & McCambridge, R. (2015). Growth lessons for nonprofits from Teach For America. Retrieved from https://nonprofitquarterly.org/2015/07/20/teach-for-america-growth-lessons-for-nonprofits/

Lubienski, C., & Brewer, T. J. (Eds.). (2019). *Learning to teach in an era of privatization: Global trends in teacher preparation*. New York, NY: Teachers College Press.

Maier, A. (2012). Doing good and doing well: Credentialism and teach for America. *Journal of Teacher Education, 63*(1), 10–22.

Millen, J. (2015). The Teach For America bait and switch: From 'you'll be making a difference' to 'you're making excuses'. Retrieved from https://www.alternet.org/2015/08/teach-america-bait-and-switch-youll-be-making-difference-youre-making-excuses/

Miner, B. (2010). Looking past the spin: Teach For America. Retrieved from http://www.dfpe.org/pdf/barbara-miner-looking-past-the-spin-teach-for-america-spring-2010.pdf

Peters, M. A. (2011). *Neoliberalism and after? Education, social policy, and the crisis of western capitalism*. New York, NY: Peter Lang.

Ravitch, D. (2015). Nonprofit quarterly: TFA has produced 25 years of hype and disappointment. Retrieved from https://dianeravitch.net/2015/09/13/nonprofit-quarterly-tfa-has-produced-25-years-of-hype-and-disappointment/

Redding, C., & Smith, T. (2016). Easy in, easy out: Are alternatively certified teachers turning over at increased rates? *American Educational Research Journal, 53*(4), 1086–1125.

Rhodes, D. (2015). Teach For America alums speak out. Retrieved from http://www.nprillinois.org/post/teach-america-alums-speak-out#stream/0

Sahlberg, P. (2012). How GERM is infecting schools around the world. Retrieved from https://www.washingtonpost.com/blogs/answer-sheet/post/how-germ-is-infecting-schools-around-the-world/2012/06/29/gJQAVELZAW_blog.html?utm_term=.ecd41f853afa

Schaefer, P. (2015). After 25 years, Teach For America results are consistently underwhelming. Retrieved from https://nonprofitquarterly.org/2015/09/11/after-25-years-teach-for-america-results-are-consistently-underwhelming/

Scott, A. (2016). College grads no longer so eager to Teach For America. Retrieved from https://www.marketplace.org/2016/03/22/world/college-grads-no-longer-so-eager-teach-america

Scott, J., Trujillo, T., & Rivera, M. (2016). Reframing Teach For America: A conceptual framework for the next generation of scholarship. *Educational Policy Analysis Archives, 24*(12), 1–33.

Stephens, T. M. (2011). Teach For America not education's cure-all. Retrieved from http://www.dispatch.com/content/stories/editorials/2011/04/06/teach-for-america-not-educations-cure-all.html

Straubhaar, R., & Friedrich, D. (2015). Theorizing and documenting the spread of teach for all and its impact on global education reform. *Educational Policy Analysis Archives, 23*(44), 1–11.

Teach For All. (n.d.). Network partners. Retrieved from https://teachforall.org/network-partners

Teran, S. (2016). Teach For America lays off its staff by 15%. Retrieved from http://www.parentherald.com/articles/32030/20160327/teach-for-america-lays-off-staff.htm

The Chronicle of Philanthropy. (2015). Teach For America debate sharpens as education corps shrinks. Retrieved from https://www.philanthropy.com/article/Teach-for-America-Debate/232701

Trujillo, T., & Scott, J. T. (2014). Superheroes and transformers: Rethinking Teach For America's leadership models. *Phi Delta Kappan, 95*(8), 57–61.

Vasquez Heilig, J., & Jez, S. J. (2010). *Teach For America: A review of the evidence.* Retrieved from East Lansing, MI: http://www.greatlakescenter.org/docs/Policy_Briefs/Heilig_TeachForAmerica.pdf

Veltri, B. T. (2010). *Learning on other people's kids: Becoming a Teach For America teacher.* Charlotte, NC: Information Age Publishing.

Veltri, B. T. (2012). Teach For America: It's more about leading than teaching. *Educational Leadership, 69*(8), 62–65.

Weiner, L. (2011). Neoliberalism's global reconstruction of schooling, teachers' work, and teacher education. In S. Tozer, B. P. Gallegos, A. M. Henry, M. B. Greiner, & P. G. Price (Eds.), *Handbook of research in the social foundations of education* (pp. 308–318). New York, NY: Routledge.

Section I Colonialism, Social Justice, Inequality, and Deficit Ideologies

1. The Non-Project

JENNY ELLIOTT

United Kingdom and South Africa

Biosketch

Jenny Elliott worked as a languages teacher in Germany, Italy and the UK before moving into Initial Teacher Education at the University of Nottingham. She worked on the Modern Languages Post Graduate Certificate in Education and was Modern Languages Lead for the Teach First East Midlands programme. She now course leads the BA Hons Education at the University of Nottingham and is the Regional Coordinator for the PGCE International in Africa.

Narrative

The first time that I heard anything about the Teach For All project was when I went to see Edith to chat to her about one of the Teach First participants that we shared. We were both tutors for the Teach First programme, working at a Russell Group university (a group of 24 self-selected research universities, perceived as being the best in the UK) and we had been working closely that year sharing the supervision of a few participants in the 2015 cohort in our capacities as subject and professional tutors. We checked in regularly with each other, giving updates on the latest lesson observation, school issues, participant crises, or their assignments. I knew vaguely that Edith was studying for a doctorate but wasn't aware of the details of her focus, or how she was getting on with it.

On one occasion Edith, who was usually quite composed and positive, appeared to be upset. I asked her whether anything was the matter and it was then that I found out the details of her doctoral project, or 'non-project,' as

Edith liked to call it. Edith's background was in teaching modern languages at secondary level and her passion was in organising linking projects. She told me that she almost hadn't accepted the offer of a job at the University, as she was reluctant to leave behind a German exchange project that she had established and run for a number of years. I'd known Edith since she started at the University in her role as tutor on the Modern Languages Post Graduate Certificate in Education (PGCE) nine years before. I had watched as she transferred her passion for the school exchange project she had left behind, into a School of Education summer voluntary project, which involved PGCE students working in township schools in South Africa for two weeks in their summer after their PGCE year. Edith had seized on this project and tried to turn it into a high-profile year-long event for the students, involving charitable fund-raising, links with local schools, videos and songs to raise awareness about our UK privilege in the face of the plights of the teachers and students in the township schools. Whilst we never actually discussed it, I knew that a few of the tutors who had been working at the University for longer, raised a quiet eyebrow at her well-meaning but slightly naïve endeavours, which filled the students with a zealous, feel-good sense of helping those less fortunate than themselves whilst actually missing some of the bigger issues such as the unequal distribution of power and the ongoing impact of colonialism.

Working in education, we get to see the transformation learning has on people's lives, identities and understandings of the world around them. This had been particularly evident to Edith as she embarked on studying her South Africa project for her Masters dissertation (at our institution, the capstone writing project for a master's degree is referred to as a dissertation while the capstone writing project for a doctoral degree is referred to as a thesis). I remember meeting her for a coffee whilst she was in the midst of her studies when she told me that she had "got it all wrong." She explained to me that the literature she had been reading about North/South educational linking projects (with 'North' meaning mainly Western, or 'developed' countries and 'South' meaning what might be called 'developing' countries) had made her feel really uncomfortable about her project in its present incarnation. She felt as though she was just reinforcing stereotypes of developing countries and White saviour roles, creating binaries of 'us' and 'them.' Ultimately, she said, the project is all about us—our CVs, photos, and do-good experience rather than about any meaningful shared interaction with the South African teachers about our lives and purposes as educators in different contexts. She went on to admit how embarrassed she now felt about the project and how she believed she needed to find a way to do it differently; so that it was meaningful for the South African teachers, too. When I asked her what a different project might look like, she explained that an ethical North/South teacher linking project worked best when the teachers were at roughly the same stage in their professional lives and when the teachers from both contexts had agreed on the purposes of their collaboration and on the aims of their project. Edith had finished our coffee conversation by letting me know that she needed to find a way to put the project right, as the business was currently unfinished. I walked away knowing that she probably would.

Not long after this, Edith moved from working on the Modern Languages PGCE to the role of Modern Languages Lead tutor for the University's Teach First programme. The University had been working with Teach First for the previous three years, albeit slightly uncomfortably, ("our principles about teacher education are just so different," a colleague had whispered to me in a meeting at the start of the collaboration). Teach First had decided to expand from offering just Maths, English, and Science at the University, and was going to offer Geography, History, and Modern Languages, which had created a new opportunity for Edith. Our paths didn't cross much for the first two years of her work on the programme, but I knew that she had graduated from her Masters programme and begun her doctorate studies. Then, we started working more closely as I was involved again in Teach First. It was at the point where I needed to talk to her about one of our participants, that I walked into her office and noticed that she had been crying. When I asked her what was wrong, she started opening up about the 'non- project.'

Starting out as a tutor on the Teach First programme and beginning her doctorate had come at the same time for Edith, and the new role and challenge had energised her. The 'unfinished business' of the PGCE South Africa project had become the focus of her doctoral research as she sought to find ways to develop the project into a mutually respectful and ethical one that was more about a meaningful teacher partnership, than a feel-good charitable holiday adventure for relatively privileged newly qualified teachers. A corridor conversation had revealed to Edith that Teach First was actually just one organisation within the wider, global network called 'Teach For All' (TFAll). At that time, TFAll was made up of 35 different organisations around the world, each with the same model for educating its beginner teachers; namely, top graduates were recruited from top universities, trained intensively for a period of a few short weeks before being placed into schools in areas of disadvantage to work full time for two years, hot-housed into leadership positions, and encouraged to commit to challenging educational inequality for the rest of their lives. Each organisation was a charity or Non-Governmental Organisation within its own context and had a number of different income streams, predominantly from local, national and international businesses wishing to associate themselves with, and support, the 'mission' of challenging educational inequality. After their minimum two-year commitment of teaching in schools, the participants were free to leave their work as teachers if they wished to. To me, the organisation sounded vaguely missionary and colonial in its purpose, zeal, and global reach, yet Edith seemed excited by it.

For her, the TFAll network provided the ideal context for the collaborative linking project that she was so keen to develop and study. It seemingly ticked all the boxes of the ethical and reciprocal collaboration she wanted to pursue. Here, at last, were teachers from the same kinds of backgrounds (strong graduates within their own contexts), at the same stages in their teaching careers, doing work that had the same principles (challenging educational inequality) in common. Edith had contacted the CEO of Teach South Africa (the iteration of TFAll in South Africa) who had been enthusiastic about his 'ambassadors' (what they call their teachers) developing an ongoing link with participants in the Teach First programme (the TFAll iteration in the UK). She had therefore decided to try to launch a new project which would encapsulate best practices in North/South teacher linking to be the focus of her doctoral thesis and give the South African and UK teachers and their classes the opportunity to develop ongoing links with one another. In Edith's eyes, it was just perfect.

Edith showed me the flyer she had produced. Having discussed it with the CEO of Teach South Africa, the decision had been made to link ten Teach South Africa ambassadors and ten Teach First participants. The project was to be named with the Zulu word 'Ubuntu' meaning 'humanity', 'compassion', or 'a person is a person through other people' to create a sense of the common, shared purpose and unity of the teachers involved. The negotiated project aims appeared on the flyer as follows:

- To gain an understanding of the global nature of teaching as a profession and the Teach For All movement;
- To gain leadership skills for developing teacher/learner international linking projects and the global citizenship dimension in your schools; and,
- To build long lasting partnerships between your schools for sharing your visions for your learners and good practice in your curriculum areas.

Teachers involved in the project were to be ambassadors in their second or third year (if they remained in teaching for a third year) of the Teach South Africa/ Teach First programme who were:

- Committed to exploring issues of social justice in education;
- Willing to attend four project meetings;

- Committed to communicating with their partner electronically (via Facebook and email) at least once a fortnight;
- Willing to develop their understanding of South Africa/the UK; and,
- Willing to visit South Africa/the UK for two weeks in their school holiday.

I could see that Edith was passionate about the Ubuntu project and that she had put a lot of time, energy and research into shaping it in a principled way that built on her previous experiences. The infrastructure appeared to be there for this to be a success. I was intrigued as to why she continued to call it a 'non-project' and why she was so upset that day.

She explained to me that she was due to fly to Johannesburg the following Thursday and that her niece was helping her to lead the project. Seven Teach First ambassadors were going to be arriving at the hostel that they were staying in, on the Friday, when they had planned to meet with the CEO of Teach South Africa. The Teach First ambassadors were going to be paired with Teach South Africa ambassadors and spend ten days in their schools around Johannesburg. It sounded exactly as she had intended so I was intrigued as to why she was so negative about it and pushed her for more detail.

Edith told me that she had tried to get someone from Teach First to co-lead the project with her but had been 'messed around.' Nigel (a pseudonym), the leader of the regional Teach First, had initially been enthused about how great the project was and how he would definitely get involved and come with her to South Africa. He and Edith had spent a whole day planning a strategy for getting funding, organising participants, and raising awareness within the wider, national Teach First network. Nigel offered to speak to contacts he had within TFAll, to let them know about the project and see if he could get financial and other in-kind support from them. But he had done nothing and all of his promises fizzled out. She had lost her temper with him by the photocopier a few months prior to this as he had said that he wouldn't be able to be involved as he was too busy. Edith had been relying on Nigel to co-lead the project with her and now needed to find somebody new. Her frustration was palpable as she told me how she had emailed the CEO of Teach First UK, the CEO of TFAll (Wendy Kopp), the Teach First research office and leads in the TFAll London office, to let them know about the Ubuntu project. The CEO of Teach First had been happy to meet to be interviewed for Edith's research, but was not in the least interested in the project when she tried to talk to him about it. Indeed, no one had shown any interest. She couldn't understand this indifference: surely the Ubuntu project encapsulated TFAll's principles of teaching as a global endeavour, with the teachers in the 'Teach For ...' organisations across the globe sharing the same purposes and ideals for themselves as teachers and for their learners and schools? Surely her project was a perfect microcosm of the global organisation? It appeared that at a local, national and international level, no one from within Teach First or TFAll really cared about Edith's project. No one wanted to join the project in a co-leading capacity, let alone support it financially, or indeed, support it at all.

Edith told me that what had kept her going was the knowledge that leaders within Teach South Africa, whilst unable to financially support the project, were enthusiastic for it to go ahead and were positively encouraging ambassadors to engage with it. "They seemed to find it much easier to get people interested in it than I did," Edith explained. "I couldn't get anybody to bloody go." Not understanding what she meant as she had clearly attracted seven people, plus her niece, to go the following week, I asked her to explain.

Reeling off the chain of events since the inception of the Ubuntu project, Edith helped me to understand what a battle she had had to get the project off the ground. Whilst there had been an initial flurry of interest when she had sent an email around to the regional Teach First ambassadors in their second year of teaching, the ten who eventually signed up for the project didn't appear to have time even to get involved in the Ubuntu project Facebook and WhatsApp group. Postings from their Teach South Africa counterparts about their daily school lives, projects that their learners were involved in and questions to the UK teachers were left unanswered. When Edith urged them to commit to hosting a Teach South Africa teacher and visiting South Africa in their summer holiday, the few that were still responding to her communications politely explained they had other commitments and could no longer be involved. This had come as a shock to Edith. When she had organised her previous South Africa project with the university's PGCE students, she had to set a cut off point for how many could be involved, as the interest was so high. Struggling to understand why there was such a lack of take-up, she sent a questionnaire out to those who had initially expressed an interest. From this, she had discovered that the financial cost of the project and the time commitment were the reasons given. Ambassadors were simply not interested in giving up their much-needed holiday time for a project that, whilst meaningful, looked like a lot of hard work. Also, they said they couldn't afford the flight and accommodation costs.

Not one to give up easily, Edith then set 'plan B' into action and had advertised the project as a 'Teach First Summer Project' to ambassadors within the wider UK Teach First network. Accepting that no financial support for the project was forthcoming from Teach First or TFAll, she had approached her University for potential pots of funding. She decided that if the funding bids were successful, she would use the money to support project flights and accommodation costs for participants who would surely now come flooding in. When she had looked at her Summer Project advertised alongside the other Teach First Summer Projects, she realised hers was rather unusual. She accepted that this was probably the reason why only three people, from different areas of the UK, had expressed an interest. The other Summer Projects offered ambassadors experience working for some of the big industry leaders and multinationals attached to Teach First as funders, whereas the Ubuntu Project was a more subtle and thoughtful professional development opportunity, which involved beginner teachers discussing shared concerns about teaching and learning as well as developing partnership projects with learners and schools. By comparison, the Ubuntu project was focused on education issues whereas the other summer projects offered to ambassadors were business oriented—supporting them to get their faces and CVs noticed within corporate networks—and appeared to be recruiting healthily. In the end, Edith scrapped the Summer Project offering as it hadn't recruited enough participants. She decided to hone her efforts again on recruiting ambassadors closer to home.

She had been delighted that her funding bid to the University had been successful and sent out an email offering £600 per successful applicant towards project costs. Her email met with no response. She then sourced further funding which enabled her to offer £1,000 per successful applicant (enough to cover all project costs including flight, accommodation and sustenance) and was relieved to receive, at last, seven expressions of interest. She had pretended that there was an application process, which interested parties needed to fulfil, but the reality was that the seven who applied were welcomed, with a secret desperation, onto the project. "I also really wanted the South Africa teachers to come to us first," Edith told me, but this had turned out to be impossible. "They struggled with the money issue, too," she said, "but I guess they have more of an excuse than we do. A flight to the UK costs about four months' salary for a typical teacher in South Africa."

It was becoming clear to me why Edith was continuing to refer to her venture as a 'non- project.' The path she had had to navigate in order to virtually coerce and bribe seven people into going to South Africa to partner with teachers for two weeks in their schools seemed unreal. 'You've made this project work,' I assured her, 'and it'll be fantastic when you are over there and when the South African teachers eventually come over here. These teachers are going to get so much out of their collaboration, it'll probably be one of the most meaningful experiences they ever have, their whole time in teaching.' I wished her all the best for the project and asked her to keep in touch with me whilst she was over there, to let me know how it was all going. I was genuinely interested to hear how it would unfold.

It was only a few days later when I had the first email from Edith in South Africa. I was glad she had her niece with her to help her to navigate through the initial shock she had.

> 4.8.16
> Hi,
> Flights all went to plan. Accommodation fine though it's FREEZING at night. Didn't pack enough socks. Students all arrived safely, so no probs there. Met with [R] and [L] from Teach South Africa to talk about the project. OMG, can't believe it. They're NOT IN Teach for All any more, apparently. Don't know what happened there, they won't say, I can't get to the bottom of it. When we started communicating two years ago, they were in TfA, just fresh back from a conference in China, but apparently they've been dropped now. MUST try to find out why before we come home. I'll keep you posted.
> How's things your end? Hope all's well,
>
> —Edith

I wondered if this had been the reason why no support had been forthcoming for Edith's project from Teach First or TFAll but then remembered she had approached them right at the start of her project plans, when presumably Teach South Africa was still a member of the global network. I was intrigued and so looked at the Teach South Africa web-site and saw that it had all the same messages about teacher education and challenging educational inequality, as all the other 'Teach for …' organisations. The structure of the teacher training was the same, too. Why was Teach South Africa no longer a part of the global network? I couldn't wait for the next update from Edith, but the next email brought no further news of the Teach South Africa mystery.

> 9.8.16
> Hi
> How are things your end? Hope all's well?
> It's so amazing here. We've been made so welcome, you wouldn't believe it. We went to TSA headquarters where they put on a reception for us with food and photos. People from all different levels of the organisation were there. Students have been paired up with teachers and put in schools. They're having great conversations about teaching and learning in their different contexts and what the challenges are. They seem to be quite surprised that the challenges are quite similar, despite different contexts, so stuff like: parental support, under-funding, lack of relevant/motivating curriculum, status of teachers and the profession as a whole, etc. I think our lot were expecting to be the experts and to have better teaching situations and whilst on the surface we have more in terms of equipment, materials, etc, a lot of the issues are actually the same. This is exactly what

The Non-Project 21

I was hoping. So the conversations are more about how these issues might be addressed with the powers that be, rather than how lucky we are in the UK cos we have 'more'. Seems much more real than the PGCE project. Also, they are really connecting and it seems that some real friendships are being forged. I feel SOOOOOOO hopeful about how they will continue when we are back in the UK. Some of the Teach South Africa ambassadors are getting their classes to do pen-friend letters/videos for their classes back in the UK. I'm so excited!!!!!

Let me know how things are going back at base. Speak soon,

—Edith

After that email, Edith clearly got very embroiled in the project, or tired, or both, as it was a while before I heard from her again. When I did, she was emailing from the airport, whilst waiting for her flight back to the UK.

17.8.16

Hi,

Sorry not to have been in touch sooner, it's been so full on. Gone well, though. A few ups and downs with some of ours who I think got a bit overwhelmed with everything and got very tired and ratty. Still, it's been very intense and we've all been living in each other's pockets to be honest, so not surprising. But on the whole it's been amazing and in some ways really quite different from the PGCE project (lots more conversations about shared issues with teaching and learning rather than us having it better etc. Also, a lot less of a focus on the poverty ('they are so poor but so happy', charity nonsense) and more on commonalities of motivating teenagers to want to do well at school in spite of curricula which don't appeal to them, etc.).

I never got to the bottom of why Teach South Africa isn't in Teach for All any more. They won't say anything about it and just hedge when I try to ask them. They have been AMAZING to us and with us, though. Honestly, organised everything so beautifully, made us so welcome. Given up loads of time when I know they are really busy. They won't commit to when they are going to return the visit, though, which is a bit frustrating, as I SOOOOOO don't want this to be one-sided, otherwise it's just like the old project. Lots of ideas for how to continue the relationship. I'm really excited about that as it means it's an ongoing project which will impact the learners on an ongoing basis, rather than a one-off escapade which ends up being all about us. Fingers crossed some really meaningful relationships will develop from this and some on-going projects. I think there will be, as there have been some real connections made between our teachers and the TSA lot. They had a great night out with lots of dancing etc. which really bonded them all. No major gossip. I'll tell you more when I'm back. Hope all's well your end. See ya soon.

—Edith

Edith was still animated from the project when we met for a coffee shortly after she got back. She was pleased with how it had gone, despite all the barriers and challenges she had had to overcome to get it going in the first place. She was intent on the next steps, which were to support the UK teachers in developing their ongoing links with their newly partnered teachers, classes, and schools in Johannesburg and to explore ways of supporting the Teach South Africa teachers with their reciprocal visit to the UK I was keen to hear how it would continue to develop and grow.

Our paths crossed less in the months that followed, though. Our University had decided to no longer work with Teach First (the contract had changed and no longer fit with the University's principles, aims, and ethos for working with beginner teachers—a difficult decision as it had meant redundancies), and Edith had moved over to a different teacher education route. She was busy writing up her thesis about the Ubuntu project for her doctorate and didn't have much time for coffees and catch-ups. The next time I saw her to properly talk to her was shortly after her graduation. She'd told me that the project had actually just fizzled out, despite all the potential for it to grow and develop. The Teach South Africa teachers weren't planning on coming to the UK. None of them could afford it and only one of them was planning on staying in teaching longer term, so they couldn't see the point in coming to visit teachers and schools in the UK when they were moving out of education. Only one of the seven UK teachers had done anything meaningful in terms of developing an ongoing link project with their Teach South Africa counterpart. Even this was going to fade away, she told me, as this UK teacher, like all of the others who had taken part in the project, was moving out of teaching and into one of the organisations Teach First was connected to. Apparently, the money and work-life balance was better in industry than it was in teaching, so very few of the Teach First ambassadors actually stayed in the classroom. Also, the jump from Teach First to the organisations they moved into was made easier by the organisation and had been positively encouraged by Teach First. I had heard this previously as one of the criticisms of the organisation but hadn't quite believed that it could be the case.

Edith seemed resigned to this state of affairs and when I asked her whether she would be trying to organise another project, she told me quietly that those days were now over. She'd believed the perfect environment for a mutual, respectful and reciprocal teacher linking project had existed within the TFAll network, and yet she still wasn't able to establish any meaningful link. Teach First and TFAll were simply not interested. Getting UK teachers to engage with it was virtually impossible as they were too exhausted from their day-to-day work in schools to give up the time in their holidays. Ongoing links were doomed, as the ambassadors did not stay in school for any reasonable amount of time to commit to such a project and to make it happen. It appeared that many of them side-stepped seamlessly into corporate jobs offered by Teach First's key funders, or they zoomed up the teaching professional ladder into leadership roles which preluded time for educational enrichment activities such as exchange projects. The very nature of the defining principles of teacher education within the 'Teach for …' organisations went against any potential long-term commitment by their teachers to their schools, their classrooms and their learners.

I eventually read Edith's doctoral thesis in which she explored the ways that the 'Teach for …' network had managed to spread so successfully and in such different contexts across the globe. She touched on what she termed 'western hegemony', where she argued that TFAll and its network of organisations was actually spreading an American model of education and teacher education, rather than responding to local idiosyncrasies in teaching and learning and different educational contexts. All of the organisations were run in the same (Western) way and with the same (Western) principles. In this respect, the North/South collaboration that Edith had been looking to explore was actually inauthentic. It could be argued it was a North/North (but in Africa) partnership where Western philosophies of colonization have become entrenched in the global export of the initial American version of TFAll, Teach For America. Whilst grappling with the reasons why Teach South Africa had initially been part of the TFAll network and then had quietly faded from its list of members by the time that she visited them for her project, Edith touched on what she thought might be a subtle, systemic racism. She had noticed that in 2017, at the time of writing her thesis, there was not a single African board member of TFAll. In fact, eight of the nine members of the TFAll 'Leadership Team' were White and all of them had been educated in institutions in the global North. She also noticed that on its web site, TFAll had a page entitled 'A Global Problem' under whose heading, every single face was Black. Perhaps an African organisation had to work harder, or had to kowtow to the overwhelmingly Western ideology underpinning TFAll, in order to be accepted in the first place, and to stay within it longer term?

Whilst she did not explicitly state it, I couldn't help but wonder whether Edith's project was perhaps doomed to fail because creating a global network of teachers with a shared purpose in challenging educational inequality was never really what TFAll was about. In my more cynical moments, I wondered whether TFAll is better understood as a neo-colonial vehicle for spreading a particular Western message about teaching and learning. Whilst doing so, it took in its wake a number of multinationals who could then quietly embed themselves within the different contexts that TFAll inhabited, quietly hoovering up the country's top graduates as they did so.

Edith finished her thesis quite aptly by describing how trying to get Teach First and TFAll interested in her project was like going to the CEO of McDonald's with her granny's apple pie recipe. The futility and hopelessness of approaching a massive multinational, which you sense has a hidden agenda quite different from that which it purports to uphold, with something that you know is real and good—the preciousness and simplicity of an individually crafted, personally meaningful offering—and having it completely ignored, came through in this analogy, and indeed, in Edith's painful accounts of her 'non-project.'

Her sense of futility and hopelessness was overbearing as I read this analogy. It captured the tenderness of her 'non-project,' like a child's home-made gift, lovingly crafted and beautiful in its imperfection and naïve confidence. It captured the cold indifference of suited backs turning and multinational doors slamming as the child turns away, still clutching the gift that was never actually wanted.

2. A Tale from the Tail of the Fish

Nickie Muir
New Zealand

Biosketch

Nickie Muir has worked teaching English as a second language in Thailand, Taiwan and Argentina and has taught English to new immigrants and refugees in New Zealand. Her syndicated column 'Inside Out' ran in the NZ Herald and Northern Advocate from 2008 to 2017. Her article; 'Northern Exposure' published in North and South investigated corruption in tertiary education in Northland. Her first children's book, (New Internationalist UK, 2014) entitled 'Baba Didi and the Godwits Fly' is a story about refugees and resilience but also about the NZ godwits and their annual migration half-way round the world. She teaches English in a public secondary school in Northland NZ where she lives with her partner and daughter.

Narrative

There are two New Zealands. I was born and grew up in the first one. The New Zealand of my childhood is the one on all the tourist brochures, with the insulated house and food on the table, trips overseas and to the museum, a pony, access to the beach and bush and an education that encouraged me to think and be an involved citizen. I then spent ten years in private international education which was well paid, educating a worldly elite who would benefit from the same cultural capital I had. Then in my 30s, after a series of personal setbacks, I found myself in one of the poorest parts of New Zealand in a mouldy rented property with a baby and a partner who couldn't speak English.

One school morning in Northland, with my new baby on my hip, I watched an eight-year-old outside my home take the cigarette out of his mouth and set fire to the contents of my rubbish bin. We'd left Argentina in the middle of a financial crisis: an IMF default where two thousand families a day sunk under the poverty line. I taught the wealthy elite of Menem's oligarchs and politicos in a private school (I even took a joy-ride in his private jet and helicopter once while teaching a group of pilots and air-traffic controllers), but I also volunteered in the local shanty town teaching street kids who couldn't afford school. I'd come 'home' to get away from the huge disparity in wealth that meant living in the same country but effectively in different worlds from those I knew in the community. Four years previously I'd gone to Argentina originally to gain the postgraduate Cambridge teaching diploma through the International House network of private schools. I'd wanted to learn Spanish and see the world and with the New Zealand dollar so weak at that time and the Argentine peso pegged to the US one, this was my best chance of doing so. Four years later the collapse in Argentina seemed imminent, I had my qualification but I was getting paid in pizza vouchers (I didn't eat pizza), and provinces like Catamarca had started printing their own currency. My contract was in pesos and the fictitious parallel with the US dollar was not going to last. I decided to come home.

I had never been to Northland before but I saw a job at the local tertiary provider 'Northtec' who were starting a new adult, first language literacy programme. I promised my new Argentine partner, an equal society where we didn't have to 'be connected' in order to get by. I told him we were proud of having one of the most equitable, corruption free societies in the developed world where children didn't have to grow up on the streets. And yet—here I was; watching this child warm himself in front of my burning rubbish bin, with a deep unease and a sense that: 'this was not my country.' A gate opened and I found myself in the second New Zealand—a country I knew nothing about with no maps or guidebook. When I went to talk to the boy—I wasn't angry, more bewildered. I offered him biscuits to stop him from running away (he was hungry), and he told me he was 'being home-schooled,' or; 'that's what I've been told to say if anyone asks me.'

He talked about his days; "Mum gave me 20 bucks for food but I spent it on a water gun and I can't go home till she's finished working." I wondered where 'setting fire to rubbish bins and talking to strangers' would fit in New Zealand's school curriculum. I also wondered what Peter Fraser would have to say about his life's work 70 years after he declared: "The Government's objective broadly expressed, is that all persons, whatever their level of ability, whether they live in town or country, have a right as citizens to a free education of the kind for which they are best fitted and to the fullest extent of their powers." I hadn't remembered New Zealand signing out of this promise—one which had not been an empty one as little as 20 years ago.

I decided not to leave Northland for a few years until I'd come to grips with, how, in this country which supposedly valued equality and social justice, we had come to this. Ten years on, I was still in Northland, a columnist for the local paper and various campaigns and sporadic outbursts of random activism later, working with disaffected youth in what is coyly termed 'alternative education.' What I discovered there, was a market driven incentive program to drop 'problem children' from the public school system where they could, or rather *had* to, be accounted for allowing schools to 'clean up' their statistics to meet Ministry pressure to improve the National Certificate of Education Achievement (NCEA) objectives. Private 'education providers' were more than willing to pick up the bounty money that came with each student from the public sector and pay untrained staff the minimum wage to babysit them. People who were sometimes severely traumatised in need of specialist care and specialised education. From here, their achievement statistics no longer existed.

I had taught in a government refugee programme in both Wellington and Auckland and worked in the tertiary sector with many refugees and new migrants. It is no exaggeration to say that I saw many of the same behaviour patterns in these children that I'd seen in Cambodian refugees I'd taught in the late '80s post Pol Pot and later with Somalian and Yugoslavian women in the '90s. These students required the most competent educators and psychologists available and instead, they had barely literate 'basketball coaches' who had themselves fallen out the education system without having achieved much. With the money from the public system—came no corresponding accountability to the community or to the education sector as to what had become of them or what they had achieved with their private education providers who had taken the public money to supposedly educate them.

Win-win. A win for the politicians and officials in the Ministry of Education as they could point to 'improved evidence based data on achievement' in the schools on their watch. A win for the schools who were obviously achieving such 'amazing' results by cherry-picking out the most at risk students and improving pass rates to an arbitrarily decided government benchmark. The businesses who picked up these children and did little with them were clipping the ticket. In order to actually educate them they would probably not have made a profit, so no incentives there to do the right thing. However, despite the leader boards outside the decile one schools in impoverished neighbourhoods declaring their '100%' pass rates—a patently ridiculous claim, it was not a win for the children who no longer had access to any form of education and who, in many cases never went to school again. And these were the children who had been expelled under due process. While the educational achievement of these children goes unrecorded and largely unmonitored the statistics for official expulsions still need to be transparent. No one likes to see a high expulsion rate. But there are a thousand ways to let a vulnerable and at risk child know that they are not wanted and that they don't belong. These conversations are often had with embarrassed family members or sometimes just the children themselves. Sometimes the child will react with embarrassment or anger and do something that would actually justify a legitimate expulsion. These children simply just walk out the gate one day and never come back. They show up on no statistics and their absence is often blamed on neglectful parenting or transitory lifestyles. This form of exclusion is so common that old hands in the education sector here refer to it as 'the Kiwi stand-down.' These are not the kinds of children who have the educated support at home who will fight for their right to an education. This was not an alternative form of education—it was an abdication of it and New Zealand education's dirty little secret. The only people clearly not winning in the deal were the kids. They were effectively being as 'disappeared' as any South American junta could engender. To be fair, I could not see how any mainstream school could cope with some of the high level behavioural, emotional, and economic needs of some of these children let alone any educational ones. Many of the children had missed years of schooling due to their transitory life-styles, a problem partially created by New Zealand's feckless adherence to the ideologies of a neoliberal unregulated rental market, with no capital gains tax. In other words: a massive, yet at that point unacknowledged by the government, housing crisis.

In the year working with these disaffected youth, I watched the privatised 'education directors,' who never showed up to teach or observe a class, buy luxury cars while trained teachers were fired and illiterate 'tutors,' offering cheap labour and asking no questions, took their place. I watched many of these young children end up as window washers or running with the gangs. I never saw the girls—the 'education' providers took the money for them but the girls never showed up and no one went looking for them. It is true that organisations like the Salvation Army did provide good care and education to a portion of these children—but for the most part 'alternative education' appeared to be a cowboy industry along the lines of the nascent business of privatising our justice and prison system. New Zealand is a country that still imprisons 17 year olds in adult jail. It wasn't a big jump from 'alternative education'—code often for being on the streets, to the local 'corrections facility.' In teaching these children, each with their own story about how they had been 'kicked out' of school I noted that most were Māori—disproportionate to the population outside the gates in that particular community. Many of them said that they felt the teachers had 'never noticed' them at school or if they did it was for things that they'd done wrong. I didn't find it surprising that this disproportionality in race was also reflected in New Zealand's prisons.

By the time the then head of the local branch of Auckland University, who had followed my column and various random acts of politics, suggested I join Teach First, I despaired that anyone was interested in the growing number of children I saw every morning happily heading out in the opposite direction to the local school. I only taught in alternative education for one year—previous to this I'd taught high-fee-paying international students in a tertiary institute situated in a low socio-economic area, and routinely saw the child (and his friends) who had set fire to my rubbish bin, outside our classroom. Twice I called him in and he sat and spoke with the international students who were horrified that so many young people were missing school in a 'first world' country. In a community of fewer than 70,000 people it was estimated that at least 2,000 children a day were out of school.

The intensity of the Summer Intensive and the romance of finding a group of like-minded professionals meant being able to name the inequity in our system in terms that had not been clear to me working at the grassroots. I had the heady sensation of having found my tribe. I was no longer paddling hard upstream alone– I had a crew and an educated and connected coxswain in the form of Teach First leadership. In the year I had spent working with youth who had been officially excluded from public secondary education I had felt very alone and was appalled that so many people in the education system knew that there was a problem but for various reasons seemed complicit in shutting down any overt conversation about addressing it. There seemed too many incentives in the system to maintain the status quo. In one case when I had complained to an auditor that there were luxury cars but no literate tutors on the books—he told me that 'as all the cars had been legitimately listed on the books—there was nothing to see here.' He did not seem interested in my point that ostensibly this was an 'education' business and therefore there should be some semblance of education happening within it. It seemed a deeply unfair and utterly insurmountable problem to address alone but one that I was equally unhappy to walk away from. On learning that Teach First wanted to work in a coordinated way to address these issues I wanted to be part of that team.

There is a euphoria in paddling in unison—no one wants to rock that boat—especially when you are exhausted; but, perhaps more importantly, no one wants to rock the boat when you all believe that you are headed in the right direction. The loyalty this engenders can become cult-like. But for me, perhaps because of my age (I was hardly the shiny new graduate at 47) or my cynicism, it wasn't long before I stopped drinking the Teach First Kool-Aid and took a good look around. It was only after I began to ask questions that did not seamlessly converge with the Teach First NZ narrative or even the popular discourse of the University we were aligned to—that I began to question some of the assumptions on which the Teach First NZ programme was based.

Leadership and Quality Teachers or Faux Elitism?

The first such assumption was that the teaching/learning crisis in New Zealand was a result of a lack of leadership and 'quality teachers' in education and not stemming from wider socio-political and economic issues allowed to develop over the last 25 years. The 'Leadership Strand,' in the Teach First NZ programme is how it recruits so many high calibre young graduates, yet the emphasis on being 'leaders' distracts attention from the larger societal picture directly impacting on classrooms. In these communities, alcohol abuse and its many societal scars, meth addiction, neglect, systemic generational educational failure, poverty, and unresolved colonial land confiscation and therefore questions of sovereignty for indigenous Māori communities, are right there with us at the chalk-face every day. The official Teach First NZ narrative was that most discussion of this fell into the category of 'deficit theorising' and was 'non-agentic.' While the hardest challenge for all of us was indeed the management of our classrooms—the opportunity to explore some of the wider pressures and look for ways our 'teaching practice' and our 'professional voice' could be formed as an agent of change, was lost. In order to be truly effective as 'constructive disrupters' we needed to understand the systems and pressures points within education and our communities. We could have learnt a lot from actual teachers working in these schools with constructive criticisms of the world we were about to enter.

These people seemed to get tarred with a 'naysayers' brush and were not welcomed into the Teach First NZ's circle. Far from being 'irrelevant' or 'non-agentic' these discussions were necessary so that we could better understand the environments we were going into and work alongside the educators who were already there—rather than set ourselves up as some great (largely White) hope.

The government discourse of the time, a government under which Teach First NZ was launched, was a neo-liberal one of 'choice.' Superficially agentic but in denial of the very real barriers that prevent people from making truly free choices or exploring ways of addressing this. To some extent, the narrative of Teach First NZ reflected this in the belief that schools could simply choose to have 'quality teachers' and 'quality leaders' and that would somehow lead to greater education equity (which first requires the assumption that veteran teachers and leaders are not of high quality). While some of the Teach First lecturers sought to balance this through their input into the programme, it became apparent that their contributions were sidelined and ceased to be the main thrust behind what was at the outset—a social justice programme aimed at addressing educational inequity.

The faux elitism of being recruited as 'quality candidates' had a dynamic of academic hegemony on top of the cultural one that is often "education" especially in the few communities where the indigenous community is in the majority. Labelling the Teach First programme as a 'leadership' programme with the emphasis on 'quality' teachers is inherently undermining and undervaluing to teaching as a profession. Some of our schools in these environments are groaning under the weight of 'leaders' and 'change agents,' an arrogant concept really suggesting that they know what needs to be changed in a community from which they don't always come from or belong. These schools sail like rudderless ships with all the ballast in the riggings. The Teach First narrative of there being a premium on 'leadership' and teaching being a temporary stepping stone to policy making and real 'change-making' positions helps to contribute to these misconceptions rather than ameliorate them. It puts new 'quality teachers' on a pedestal and then expects the very people it is comparing them with to mentor them in a spirit of generosity. Over the last 4 years I have witnessed non-Teach First teachers achieving stellar results, often without support or acknowledgement, who are not promoted to leadership positions because they are invaluable in the classroom, and so, never receive the kudos or authority which they deserve. If supported, they could affect real change *without having to leave the classroom*. Teach First NZ (TFNZ) needs to consider reframing the narrative so that TFNZ recruits are these teachers' apprentices—not their future 'quality leaders.'

In fairness to Teach First, there is undoubtedly a great need for more teachers in our low decile schools and anything that could provide that should be welcomed. More than a few secondary schools in Northland have no permanent Maths, Science, or English teachers in front of students. Plenty of leaders though. It's not immediately apparent where any of the leaders are taking us mortal teachers or our charges to, nor what the philosophy behind any of the changes they are making are based upon. Despite the endless 'student voice' surveys, there is little real evidence that students or community are ever genuinely consulted on what they consider 'good schooling' or 'an education' or how they want it delivered. There is even less 'teacher voice' especially from those teachers who have lived in these communities for many years and are often doing amazing work against all conceivable odds.

In placing a higher value on a new cohort of Teach First teachers, recruited outside of the community, there is an elitism not based in reality that is the antithesis of an equity agenda. These communities, especially in Northland, are highly sensitive to this reality. As one union rep and ex-principal said to me; "If you guys are the quality teachers—what are we? Chopped liver?" Many of these teachers have a far more realistic idea of what it would take to create positive change than someone riding in on a magical rainbow with a cavalry of unicorn ponies loved up on pixie dust from the Summer Intensive. When I told TFNZ I would wear the logoed t-shirt which read: "Teach First: Lead the Way!" to school events only if I really wanted to get shanked by my colleagues, they laughed. This would only have been funny if I had been joking.

Education Is Good, NCEA and 'The Tail'

Northland is, in Te Ao Māori: 'Te Hiku' or 'The Tail' (of the Fish of Māui). There is a saying that 'the head won't move until the tail does' meaning that you can't affect change at the head—or Wellington; i.e., parliament—until the North moves. It's a nice idea but for most of the nearly 20 years I've lived here we just always seem to be the tail in every statistic. Northland is constantly measured among the worst in youth justice, truancy, and education achievement rates in the country; yet, very little work has been done into exploring why that might be, rather we continue to push the idea that if teachers work harder at getting better pass rates in NCEA then our communities will magically be transformed.

'Gapping it' or 'Ditching' (bunking class) seems to be an NCEA subject in itself in this part of New Zealand. One morning I had a class bail out a window to go swimming and was told this was just 'poor classroom management' on my behalf, which to be fair, was probably true. My instinct however was that this was also a perfectly legitimate response by intelligent human beings to an intolerable situation: I was the fourth teacher –and a 'beginner one' at that, in as many months—their science teacher, their seventh. This attitude was taken by Teach First as 'non-agentic.' Seeing 'disengagement' as a positive active reaction to appalling education systems measuring irrelevant benchmarks for these children, was not part of the Teach First discourse.

There was an inherent assumption from TFNZ that 'education is good.' But what if New Zealand's delivery of public education in some of these communities had been universally appalling (with the obvious exception of those previously mentioned exceptional teachers), possibly for generations? Should we be trying to gain better achievement rates in a system if the Teach First argument in the first place was that the education system was 'broken'? What if the education system was not in fact broken but the key stakeholders (the students) had no actual stake in any of the outcomes? What if things like performance bonuses for principals for achieving arbitrary percentage pass rates, were killing education in these communities? Especially when internally assessed credits, equally valid for possum trapping as for physics incentivised whole communities to not be learning maths, science or gaining basic literacy. Could it be that the need to reach Ministry benchmarks in any way possible on the one hand and maintain some form of educational standard on the other, were two opposing tectonic political pressure plates and students and their teachers were getting crushed in the middle? What if NCEA was killing education? And what if kids from very impoverished communities simply start the race 100 leagues behind and need other (sometimes expensive) things in order to play catch up? All questions to which the answer is hardly novice teachers with a few short weeks of training.

'I Am Sovereignty'

If TFNZ really is an agent of radical education reform, should it instead be aiming to break the systems that had arguably 'broken' some of these school communities in the first place? Would it mean actively taking on the alcohol and gambling corporations and lobbyists that prey on our poorest school communities? Would it consider what the delivery of a 'decolonised' curriculum might look like?

Despite having some excellent university lecturers, the post-colonial context was not really explored or understood by TFNZ management and I would suggest that it would be even less well understood by Mindlab, a private education business, who have now taken over the teaching component of the programme, replacing the University of Auckland relationship with TFNZ. Unpacking and exploring those concepts would mean a very different understanding of what 'leadership' might look like in the Teach First organisation itself.

There was also a lack of understanding of what it is for Pakeha, white New Zealanders, to be working post-Treaty and pre-settlement in a post-colonial era. The Treaty of Waitangi is, especially for Māori, New Zealand's founding document and still the source of much contention in New Zealand today. It laid the base for the relationship between the two races. Much was lost (and gained) in the translation of that document, effectively creating two different documents that had different interpretations of ownership and sovereignty. The 500 odd Māori chiefs that signed the Treaty in their own language maintained that they never gave over their sovereignty to the Crown. Much that was well intended and signed in good spirit was not adhered to by the colonial government and over the course of nearly 200 years most Māori entitlement to land was lost. Many Māori families today, especially in Northland are actively involved in the reparation or settlement process where the Crown (represented by the government) apologizes for past transgressions and gives back a small percentage of the land and the monetary equivalent of what was taken away. Some tribes around New Zealand have already settled and the process of forgiveness, understanding and healing is underway. This is not the case in Northland—perhaps because it was first to be colonised, in many ways it was hardest hit and many Māori children who have sat through the years of hearings, and watched great-grandparents and grandparents pass away still fighting for resolution, will have heard the stories of the shrewd, the cruel and the clearly unforgivable in terms of how their ancestral lands and fishing and forestry rights were taken. These stories are hardly ever heard by Pakeha and are not taught in our school curriculum. Much of this land had at one time been gifted by Māori to the Education Department or to local councils for schools and parks. Some of the people who were involved in taking the land or benefitted from the cheap sale of it, also sat on local school boards and councils. Some of these deals were still being done in the 1960s and 1970s under the Public Works Act and some of the people who lost their land under those deals are still alive today. To say that there is resentment of those in authority here, which includes schools, would be an understatement. New Pakeha teaching recruits coming into these mainstream schools where over 90% of the population is Māori, without a very thorough and specific understanding of the Treaty of Waitangi and the history of the region, will experience resentment and at times raw aggression without seeing where it is actually aimed. My experience of having my 11-year-old daughter in the school with me; was that she was treated to warm and inclusive hospitality and friendship by the same children who, at first, treated me, as their teacher with utter disregard. It took me more than a few months to understand that this resentment was not actually about me or anything I was or wasn't doing in the classroom. It had everything to do with what they thought I stood for.

 The context for those of us who were in the poorest regions of the Far North was so different to those experienced by the tutors and most of the trainees that we as a group stopped discussing them outside of our own core group because we were either not believed when we reported what was evident 'in the field' or because we were simply labelled as 'not resilient' or 'non-agentic' enough to cope. In other words, our questions regarding our experience suggested 'failure.' If the actual work many of us did in these communities was measured I think this assumption was far from true but these labels served to silence us and prevented us from examining collectively, ways of addressing some of the issues we faced.

For many communities in the Far North, education equals a loss of sovereignty. Education equals neo-colonisation. Unless students specifically study New Zealand history in their senior years or individual teachers are conscientious about incorporating local stories and culture into their teaching or ask students for their own knowledge of these things—there is nothing in the curriculum that reflects our pre-colonial and early colonial foundations or current cultural realities. Many Pakeha children will not know the word 'sovereignty.' There is a reason however why a class of Year 11 Māori students with an operating vocabulary of fewer than 2,000 common words in English knew the word 'sovereignty.' It is a cornerstone of the Treaty and our road map for relationship between two peoples. In a poem titled 'I am sovereignty' one student listed all the things Pakeha had brought to the North. It included 'booze, syphilis, and schooling.' In that order. 'To get schooled' in the vernacular here, is to get a punitive authoritarian telling off—or even a beating. It is the opposite of dialogue. A 'scholar' is a dismissive term of abuse for those who are seen to be 'suck ups' at school. Doing too well academically can be seen by some groups as being a sell-out. Before assuming 'education is good' or that increasing NCEA pass rates is the measurement of all success we might need to ask a few questions about what a 'good education' might mean to the people 'getting schooled' or whether or not 'we' are even the right people to be 'schooling' anyone.

During the 2014 Summer Intensive, the Waitangi Tribunal investigating settlement claims found that local Māori chiefs never ceded sovereignty to the Crown when they signed the Treaty. This was of 'huge significance' to Ngāpuhi—the overarching tribe of Northland. By that evening the government negotiator Mr. Chris Finlayson had shut down the conversation with this declaration: "Every New Zealander goes to bed tonight knowing that Her Majesty reigns over us and the Government rules." It is difficult to believe that this sentence came from this century from an independent nation state and is indicative of how little has changed in those nearly 200 years since colonisation. Because what he really meant was: 'every Pakeha New Zealander.' I would hazard a guess that many Māori New Zealanders went to bed knowing the exact opposite. That is, that what they had always attested to be the truth, had finally been acknowledged. They may also have held the hope of a shift in mindset as a country leading to the address of many of the social issues arising from systemic inequity. Until Teach First NZ (and now, Mindlab) comes to grips with history and the Treaty, the realities of why some communities are fundamentally resistant to 'education' will remain elusive and our practice is unlikely to ever do more than just reinforce the status quo.

Field Scholars Go Bush

Despite being 'field-based' scholars, an exciting epitaph plastered on our post-graduate diplomas, there appeared to be few in the organisation who were genuinely interested in our 'field' or our 'notes' of the Far North or could help us grapple with the very real and at times confronting situations we found ourselves in. Often in order to attempt to meet our TFNZ mandate of working towards increased equity for students we ended up working against directives from senior management within the schools. It became clear that in many schools some students were not asked to participate in external examinations, perhaps being seen as; 'a risk to the school statistics.' If mentees were told to only enrol those students who 'were ready' to sit the exam, and if that was fewer than 20% of the class—those who were sure to pass, this might be considered inequitable by the Teach First mentee. If she then goes and enrols 100% of the students in the exam, gets a huge leap in participation and engagement with the concept of exams, but the achievement data drops as a result—she is then potentially following the indications of TFNZ leadership and yet directly in conflict with her daily line manager. If Teach First NZ as an organisation is unwilling or unable to support, advise and actively participate in these conversations it is a very lonely and potentially dangerous place for TFNZ recruits to be placed. It is a very tall order for a new teacher with only 6 weeks teaching practice under her belt.

I am a natural dissenter—it was how I found my way to Teach First in the first place. I wanted to understand why so many of our brightest and most creative offspring were being excluded from the institution trusted to ensure they flourish, namely, public education in Aotearoa. It was not that I disagreed with Teach First NZ's suggestion that New Zealand has a massive issue with educational inequity and that it is imperative that this be addressed— I still don't. It was that the discourse within the organisation was not robust enough to encompass sufficient dissent or to listen carefully enough to those in the field whose field notes were beginning to show a different narrative from what Teach First NZ had dictated. A lack of equitable

'Freirean dialogue,' if you like, and if this discourse was not offered to participants how then could this be modelled in the communities we then went out to serve (or rather: 'lead'?)

Teach First NZ has yet to address the mismatch in perception between the programme recruiting 'elite' or 'quality' candidates as future leaders and what some in senior management see as a cost-effective way of addressing the chronic teacher shortage. I asked one senior manager recently if his school was going to have Teach First candidates in the coming year. "We would love to have lots of them!" he answered, "because they're so damn cheap." I sat there, a stunned mullet gasping for air. While the government does pay the salary of Teach First NZ teachers they require 5 hours a week of a senior teacher's teaching time in order to mentor them. When I pointed out that as he had only one secondary trained teacher who could teach senior curriculum in that department and therefore they could ill afford the hours taken up in mentoring—he gave a shrug and rolled his eyes. The implication seemed to be that the Ministry would pay their wages and we would get reasonably competent human beings in front of the smaller humans. Why was I making a fuss? Hell, we're a small low decile school in Northland—they might not get the mentoring because we needed the mentors actually teaching—but who will ever know? As he walked off, I had pause to reflect that these types of leadership decisions are just one more way New Zealand could turn itself into a banana republic without the benefit of having any actual bananas.

On Blowing Up Bridges—Constructive Disruption or Faux Activism?

Along with the faux elitism of being 'quality teachers or leaders' I also had a problem with the faux activism and lack of collegiality that the label of being 'change-makers,' suggests. In my first years at university I had a delightful Indian political science lecturer who found us to be as representative of wild student radicalism in the first phase of New Zealand's experiment with neo-liberalism as a bunch of turnips. He came in one morning ranting, "I cannot believe you would be letting them get away with any of this ... if this were India ... you would have been setting fire to bridges and blowing up the post offices."

Having taught the children of war as refugees accepted under the quota system in New Zealand, I am cured of thinking that violence is the answer to anything but a failing economy, but there is always room for high grade, coordinated and systemic disruption. Especially when the equity balance is so far tipped that those on the bottom need crampons and climbing ropes to even get close to a level playing field of attaining an equitable public education. I still hold hope that Teach First will remain a significant contributor to this disruption but also know the test of this is the ability of the organisation to listen to the communities and teachers who work in them—which, to date, they have not accomplished. They will need to value our non-Teach First colleagues, over 'leaders' as the engine room of change in education. There is yet to be a vigorous 'bridge burning' conversation around whether or not NCEA is in fact killing learning and education in New Zealand and is any 'good' or whether the measurements we use to judge 'success' in Teach First and NZ education in general are even relevant. The discussion around whether Teach First (or now, Mindlab in place of Auckland University) as an organisation, especially with respect to its board and leadership is not just another hegemonic organisation that has not really come to terms with the kaupapa of a multicultural, much less bicultural, society and what that might look like in terms of educational and political disruption of the status quo is yet to be had. There are also the awkward conversations that need to be had around funding and corporate sponsorship which are difficult to question when it is not always apparent where money is coming from. It is difficult to retain integrity if you are working for a social justice organisation that is funded by the same oil company that the people whose kids you are teaching, are desperately trying to fight.

When the parameters of the conversation are ample enough to sustain considered and constructive dissent that may, in the end threaten the organisation's very existence, then I hold hope that Teach First may indeed be a significant contributor to addressing the terrible inequity that continues to blight New Zealand's education system.

Glossary

Aotearoa: New Zealand
Kaupapa: Issue/Theme
NCEA: National Certificate of Educational Achievement
Pakeha: White New Zealander
Shanked: prison or gang slang for being stabbed with a knife
Te Ao Māori: The Māori world /worldview
To Go Bush: Go rogue/off the beaten track/out of the field and out the gate ...
Te Hiku: The Tail is a local name for Northland. It comes from the story of Maui fishing a great fish from the ocean which is the North Island. Wellington is the head and Northland the tail.

3. Disparities Between Expectations and Impact in Fellows' Experience of an Alternative Teaching Program in China

YUE MELODY YIN AND HILARY HUGHES
China

Biosketch

Yue Melody Yin obtained her PhD in the Faculty of Education at Queensland University of Technology, Australia. She specializes in the sociology of education. Her research topic is about the alternative teacher recruitment programs which channel prestigious university graduates to the teaching profession in disadvantaged schools.

Hilary Hughes is Adjunct Associate Professor at the Faculty of Education Faculty, Queensland University of Technology, Australia. She is an experienced educator-researcher with particular interest in international student experience, learning environment design, informed and connected learning, and libraries. In 2010 Hilary was Fulbright Scholar-in-Residence at University of Colorado Denver.

Narrative

Introduction

Teach For All (TFAll) programs in several countries, including China, recruit high achieving university graduates into the teaching profession. Although these graduates are often well qualified to pursue alternate careers which provide better pay, as teaching fellows they commit to working in disadvantaged schools with seemingly less appealing geographic and socio-economic locations (Olmedo, Bailey, & Ball, 2013; Straubhaar & Gottfried, 2016). Alternative teacher training and employment programs have been researched in developed western countries, such as the United States, the U.K., and Australia (La Londe, Brewer, & Lubienski, 2015; Muijs, Chapman, & Armstrong, 2013; Skourdoumbis, 2012). Little attention, however, has been paid to similar initiatives in China. Moreover, there is limited understanding about the graduate recruits' experience of teaching in the challenging and often unfamiliar social contexts in which they find themselves. Therefore, this chapter discusses select findings from a mixed methods study that explored the transition of 14 graduates from prestigious Chinese universities becoming teaching fellows in disadvantaged schools through a program designated here as Exceptional Graduates as Rural Teachers (EGRT)[1] (Yin, 2018). The aim of the study was to develop understanding of EGRT fellows' transition experience through the sociological lens of Bourdieusian theory, rather than to critique or compare particular alternative teaching programs. The findings presented here reveal significant disparities between the fellows' pre-service expectations and perceived impacts of their teaching through the EGRT program.

This chapter comprises six main parts which cover: context of EGRT in China; previous research; the study's sociological lens; the research design; findings; and discussion of implications.

Exceptional Graduates as Rural Teachers (EGRT)

China has developed an "urban priority and urban oriented" pattern for accelerating modernization and industrialization since the founding of the People's Republic of China in 1949 (Rao & Ye, 2016, p. 601). Consequently, the rural-urban education gap is rapidly widening. This structural disadvantage is a source of national concern; in the media, rural students have long been depicted as children who yearn for knowledge and are keen to learn. Images usually show these children as school-hungry students with big and shining eyes. As a result, a widely-accepted stereotypical impression of rural students is that these children are eager to learn but are constrained by limited educational opportunities and lack of qualified school teachers.

As a means for addressing this problem, more than one thousand teachers recruited through alternative programs such as have worked in disadvantaged schools (Year 1–Year 9) since 2008. About 300 schools have been involved in EGRT as placement schools, located in the underdeveloped rural areas of five provinces of China. The program promotes a vision that every child deserves a good education and conceptualizes teaching as a form of leadership. Guided by this vision, EGRT offers empowering opportunities for personal leadership to recruits, who are expected to have transformative and life-long impacts on students in disadvantaged schools. EGRT marketing apparently intends to attract individuals who are seeking a different life trajectory and have the ambition of doing something extraordinary (Yin, Dooley, & Mu, 2019). These rhetorical promotion strategies reflect those of "Teach For ..." programs in other countries. In addition to the marketing strategies, EGRT provides about six weeks' pre-service training named Summer Institute. This type of short-term training has been widely criticised by scholars in the relevant research about other Teach for programs (Anderson, 2013; Brewer, 2014).

Previous studies in many countries have shown significant disparities between teachers' expectations and the realities of working in disadvantaged schools. Graduates tend to be highly idealistic, which does not prepare them well for the reality of working in disadvantaged communities (Crawford-Garrett, 2017). They often experience a mismatch between their expectation of innocent students with a strong desire for knowledge and the reality of disaffected students who are seemingly reluctant to learn. This mismatch can cause frustration and depression by failing to satisfy teachers' altruistic desire to motivate students in disadvantaged schools (Ingersoll, 2003; McCann, Johannessen, & Ricca, 2005; Zhou & Shang, 2011). Teachers reportedly feel extremely frustrated when their willingness to make a difference in disadvantaged schools seldom receives a positive response from students (Boyd, Lankford, Loeb, & Wyckoff, 2005). These findings suggest that teachers cannot obtain a great sense of achievement and satisfaction when students are less interested in learning and are achieving lower academic performances than the teachers had expected (Lampert, Burnett, & Davie, 2012). Consequently, students' lower academic achievement can discourage and exhaust teachers, which can result in high attrition rates among teachers (McCann & Johannessen, 2005; Zhou & Shang, 2011).

A key disparity between expectation and reality relates to teachers' limited understanding of the social context of the children they teach. It has a significant impact on how teachers understand students' performance and interpret their own frustration at work (Schaffer, White, & Brown, 2016). As Yiu and Adams (2013) pointed out, teachers working in rural areas, especially those from urban backgrounds, tend to hold preconceived notions of rural students having limited ability and future life chance based on stereotypical assumptions about gender, socio-economic status, and school type. The EGRT study, however, showed that prior to their service the graduate teachers usually believe that students in disadvantaged schools have the potential to be changed. This belief seems to derive less from sociological recognition of students in disadvantaged schools and desire to contradict the effects of deficit discourse, than from strong confidence in their own ability to make a difference. When their personal impact did not perform as anticipated, they usually blamed the students through deficit discourse (Yin, 2018).

Sociological Lens: Capital and Habitus

The EGRT study drew upon the sociological theory of Pierre Bourdieu in order to examine the disparities between the fellows' expectations and perceived impact as teachers. Capital refers to all material or symbolic resources worth being pursued and possessed. Capital is the potential to produce profits and to reproduce itself in identical or extended forms within particular social contexts (Bourdieu, 1986). EGRT fellows, as graduates from prestigious domestic and international universities, are endowed with privileged cultural and symbolic capital (Bourdieu, 1986) which is celebrated in the labour market of contemporary China. Cultural and symbolic capital refers to knowledge (amongst other things) and reputation recognised in a particular social space. With accrued cultural and symbolic capital EGRT fellows have the potential to place themselves in a favourable social position given their "position taking" (Bourdieu, 1983, p. 312) to earn economic capital (e.g., money, property). In contrast, owing to the unequal distribution of educational resources in China, students in disadvantaged rural schools lack economic capital and cultural capital compared with their urban counterparts and may be classified as having a deficit in social and cultural capital. Correspondingly, this results in the rural students lagging behind in both current academic performance.

The difference of EGRT fellows and their rural students is not only demonstrated in terms of capital, but also habitus. Habitus is another important concept proposed by Bourdieu, which is a system of social classification:

> In the form of a system of classification, the mental and bodily schemata that function as symbolic templates for the practical activities—conduct, thoughts, feelings, and judgement—of social agents. (Bourdieu & Wacquant, 1992, p. 7)

Thus, habitus identifies characteristic or habitual practices such as speaking, walking, eating, gesturing and thereby feeling and thinking (Bourdieu, 1990). For example, in this study, an EGRT fellow's habitus might be associated with elite education, sophisticated urban values, perceptions of modern life styles, and thinking modes. According to Bourdieu and Wacquant (1992), social structures and mental structures are homologous and genetically linked. The objective division and differentiation of society, particularly the grouping of the dominant and the dominated, affect subjective awareness of individuals. As social agents they are constantly exposed to the extant social context, and they internalize its logics of typology. Thus, the mental scheme is the product that social divisions embody in social agents' dispositions.

In other words, classification involves a system of "principles of vision and division" (Marom, 2014, p. 1909) which works in delineating a situation, grouping, and interpreting a social phenomenon. Social agents usually tend to unconsciously apply these principles in daily life when schemes of thought find instant adherence to "the world of tradition experienced as a natural world" (Bourdieu, 1977, p. 164). These social realities seem unquestioned and self-evident. Accordingly, socially constituted classificatory schemes are easily legitimated as necessary and natural by the dominant group. Then the social classification produced by the current social structures constructs the internal order of social agents. In this situation, the dominated groups who take the unprivileged social positions with limited resources are easily classified as inferior in the perceptual scheme of classification and stigmatised in the dominant discourse (Bourdieu, 1984). Therefore, this chapter situates graduates from prestigious universities as having favourable capital in both amount and configuration constitute the dominant group, while students in disadvantaged schools become the dominated group. Deficit discourse labels those students as vulnerable and at-risk due to a perceived lack of social and cultural capital.

Research Design

Yue (the chapter's lead author) conducted the research and visited six disadvantaged schools in rural China to interview 14 EGRT fellows in total. Invitations were sent via a brief survey to current fellows at an EGRT event. The 14 participants were selected from a pool of volunteers based on their demographic diversity (See Table 3.1). They participated in individual semi-structured interviews at their placement schools. Open-ended questions and probing questions encouraged extended responses. The interviews were conducted in Mandarin, transcribed, and then translated into English. All interview participants were given pseudonyms. Thematic analysis was applied to the collected data, as it is regarded as a fundamental method for qualitative data analysis, and even as a sort of shared genetic skill among qualitative data analysts (Braun & Clarke, 2006; Holloway & Todres, 2003). This process enabled themes to emerge, with each one "captur[ing] something important about the data in relation to the research question, and represent[ing] some level of patterned response or meaning with the data set" (Braun & Clarke, 2006, p. 82). Furthermore, Bourdieu's theory informed the deductive analytical framework.

Table 3.1. The demographic characteristics of interview participants.

Name	Gender	Age	Secondary school	University	Degree	Family origin
Wei	Male	25	Key	985 Project	Bachelor	urban
Zhao	Female	24	Key	985 Project	Bachelor	urban
Xiu	Female	24	Key	985 Project	Bachelor	urban
Shuang	Female	23	International	Overseas university	Bachelor	urban
Xiang	Male	24	Key	985 Project	Bachelor	urban
Feng	Male	27	Key	985 Project	Masters	urban
Sun	Male	30	Key	985 Project	Doctorate	urban
Min	Female	23	Non-Key	211 Project	Bachelor	fringe
Ying	Female	22	Key	985 Project	Bachelor	rural
Na	Female	24	Key	985 Project	Bachelor	rural
Rui	Male	28	Key	Non-211/985 Project	Bachelor	rural
Hua	Female	27	Key	985 Project	Masters	rural
Ren	Female	27	Key	985 Project	Masters	rural
Long	Male	27	Key	985 Project	Masters	rural

While the complete interview protocol explored EGRT participants' whole experience as teachers in disadvantaged rural schools, this chapter focuses on findings about the participants' expectations and perceived personal impact, as discussed in the following section.

Findings: Disparities Between EGRT Fellows' Expectations and Perceived Impact

While the 14 EGRT participants were all graduates of prestigious universities, they had diverse personal and academic backgrounds. They had grown up in differing urban and rural settings (see Table 3.1).

Based on the collected data, these fellows experienced disparities between their pre-service expectations and reality of their impact as teachers in disadvantaged rural schools. These disparities, which related to the limited scope and sustainability of their impact, generated negative emotions for the fellows.

When asked "up to now, to what extent has your impact reached your expectations?" most interview participants (11 of 14) stated that they were disappointed—sometimes desperate—when they thought about the limited difference they had made, or the durability of such difference. This negative response contrasts with the EGRT promotional rhetoric claiming that fellows are expected to have a transformative and life-long impact on local students within and beyond the academic domain. The fellows came to a gradual realization that their limited impact on students' education mismatched their pre-service assumptions. As Zhao confided:

> I racked my brains solving this education inequality but ended up with much disappointment, defeat, and despair. Maybe I really can't solve the problem. I can only make a really small change but can't solve the problem at all.

Zhao perceived that she was not able to make as much change as she had thought she would. She initially believed that she could bring transformative difference to local students with her constant striving as a hero. This belief seems to accord with saviour narratives, usually held by a privileged group who view poverty as a "rurality" to be solved rather than identified any local strength (Smart, Hutchings, Maylor, Mendick, & Menter, 2009). However, she later realized that her previous thoughts were unrealistic. This was not an individual plight, as Lam (2017) revealed that Teach For China fellows in her study fell into a similar dilemma when they lacked adequate and effective training to navigate the real classroom. As a result, Zhao gave up her ambition to make a dramatic difference in the face of entrenched educational inequality. During this process, many negative emotions, such as "disappointment, defeat, and despair," were generated. The responses of Zhao and other participants align with research findings that emotion is not only associated with an individual's current situation, but also with perceived possibilities (Lin, 2012). Thus, the mismatch between Zhao's anticipated and actual outcomes generated a strong emotional response. Such experience was not uncommon amongst the interview participants. While Zhao talked about her helplessness in terms of changing educational equality, a relatively abstract concept, others described disparities in a more applied way, mainly in terms of the scope of their impact. For example, Wei, Ying and Hua had assumed that they could have a wide-ranging impact on local education.

Wei's ambition was to have an impact on the whole school. He expected his placement school could be changed because of his coming. Then he realized the reality was far from his expectations:

> I previously imagined changing the school, however, I realized how unrealistic I had been after working here.

Ying assumed that she could exert impact not only on local students but also on local teachers. However, the reality was that her impact might have only been felt on local students. She confessed that her impact on local teachers was negligible:

> I indeed had some impact but not to the degree I imagined. The impact I thought at the beginning was to influence not only my students but also all [local] teachers, to help them continuously gain a positive attitude towards learning, to change them. However, I gradually understood local teachers and they had almost tried their utmost.

Hua just focused on her efforts on local students, expecting to influence the majority of them; but she noticed that maybe just one or two students listened to her words:

> When I talked with them [local students] about things like responsibility and perseverance, I had to admit the fact that not all of them could be influenced. My impact might even just reach one or two [students], which was so different from what I had expected.

According to the above excerpts, Ying was trying to enculturate local teachers with a similar mindset to her own, such as a "positive attitude towards learning," while Hua was imparting values like "responsibility and perseverance." They seemed to believe that their own attitudes and values should be adopted by local teachers and students who they tended to regard as having negative attitudes and lack of perseverance. From a sociological perspective, their habitus led them to categorize local people and themselves into different groups; and the local teachers and students became the group that should improve and change. This reflected how middle or upper-class values and stereotypes towards the dominated group were reproduced (Smart et al., 2009). These pre-reflexive classificatory schemata (Bourdieu & Wacquant, 1992) seemed to create disparities when the fellows' efforts were resisted by local teachers and students.

These disparities related to pre-reflexive classificatory schemata might be rooted in differing experience in the educational space of EGRT fellows and local teachers. While the local teachers had relatively low academic credentials and prestige, EGRT were highly qualified participants who had first won the fierce battle of the Chinese College Entrance examination to become members of prestigious universities. They then competed again successfully, against many peers, for involvement in EGRT. As exceptional graduates from prestigious universities, they had cultural and symbolic capital which could open access to power and influence. Following Tamir's (2009) argument, these elite graduates were widely viewed by the public as young talents with potential for leadership, excellence and distinction, which led to a perception that "views elite college graduates as fully entitled to authority and power"

(p. 538). Thus, the EGRT fellows believed that they should and could exert an impact on, and even change others, as promoted by EGRT rhetorical strategies in both its marketing and training process.

In addition to the scope of their impact, participants expressed concern about the sustainability of their impact. For example, Sun stated:

> I taught students in Grade Six and now they have entered junior high school. Although some students performed fairly well after they went to study in the town, others did not. I did not know whether it was because I didn't do enough or my impact was not strong enough. They [some students] stay in this [local] secondary school where education quality was very bad. Through chatting with them, I found they've gradually returned to the original point and felt good staying in this small village and playing with people they know. They had made some changes before, but now these changes disappeared after they graduated and left me. I talked to them about the outside world and they felt it not interesting. They were not thinking about something beyond. It was a pity for them, especially those with great potential.

Revealing concern about the sustainability of his impact, Sun believed his students did make some positive changes which he brought about. Due to his impact, some local students began to study hard and change their attitudes toward the outside world. However, this impact was not sustained. The word "return" was very telling. Some students went back to where they were without any desire for the outside world or for the corresponding diligence they had acquired through Sun's efforts. That is to say, Sun only made a positive difference on local students for a limited period. This made him frustrated.

Other interview participants (Feng, Long, Wei, Xiang, Zhao, Long and Rui) expressed similar concerns about the fact that their impact on students was not as sustainable as they had expected. This phenomenon could be explained by the concept of habitus proposed by Bourdieu. Students' views of the world and their dispositions had been formed on the basis of their previous upbringing and learning experiences. These habitual views and dispositions were durable. Although habitus was a system open to change, the previous habitus still had a great influence in orienting individuals' behaviours (Bourdieu, 1993). Students might participate in some new practice introduced by fellows, but this did not mean that their habitus was changed (Dooley, Exley, & Poulus, 2016).

Since the vision of EGRT was that every child deserves a good education, the desired transformative and life-long impact was expected to function on each student in the classroom. This was much harder to realize than the fellows assumed before, however, and consequently frustrated them when in service. In this situation, fellows tried to make sense of their own efforts and contributions in terms of their personal impact scope and sustainability. When frustrated by realities, fellows tried to justify their hard work from other perspectives. Take Xiang, for instance:

> I just imagined I was a boy who walked along the beach on evening at low tide. Thousands of starfish had been stranded on the sand by the receding waters. I tried to pick up as many as possible to throw back to the sea. Although I knew what I did could not change the whole picture, it made sense for each individual one.

Xiang's initial intention seemed idealistic and reflected a saviour narrative (Smart et al., 2009) but over time he came to the practical realisation that he could not support all students. He then revised the scope of his impact, by paying attention to the students who had been influenced. Just like the imagined boy, he could not save all starfish, but his efforts meant so much for the few who he had saved. As for the sustainability of their impact, Shuang figured out a good metaphor:

> Although I was frustrated by local students' easily bouncing back to their previous level of academic performance, I believed that I sowed good seeds in their heart, and these seeds might sprout and flourish one day.

Shuang reasoned that the education she provided for students was like seeds, so that the educational effect might not be presented immediately, but it did not necessarily mean that her efforts were in vain.

The above excerpts from Xiang and Shuang show how fellows comforted themselves when confronted by the perceived disparities of personal impact in terms of both scope and sustainability. The lack of sufficient training largely contributed to this sense of helplessness. Although such accounts seem like self-consolation, they were important to the EGRT fellows in giving the inner energy to continue their work in face of various difficulties and to offset negative feelings of the perceived disparities of personal impact. These strategies might work in practice and even contribute to shaping individual fellows' resilience, however, deeper understanding of the sociological roots of such disparities is crucial to enhancing the development and ongoing support of EGRT fellows, as discussed in the following section.

Sociological Perspectives of the Disparities

The disparities between EGRT fellows' expectations and actual experience of teaching in disadvantaged rural schools, as outlined above, tended to generate negative emotions, such as disappointment, depression or even desperation. These emotions appeared to be associated with deficit thinking which was pervasive in their interview response. Deficit thinking was evident in: (1)

media promotion; (2) advertisement strategies employed by EGRT; and (3) classification schemata of the fellows' habitus which was shaped by social changes in the past decades.

First, the media widely promotes a belief in China that rural students want to learn but are constrained by unequal opportunities. This view is presented by powerful national broadcasters like China Central Television and People's Daily, text books, social media, and public awareness campaigns (Zhou & Shang, 2011). Extensive promotional campaigns include the Hope Project, an anti-poverty educational project, and the Development of the Western Region Initiative. All these media and campaigns play a pivotal role in arousing emotional empathy and a desire for social justice in the public. A stereotyped impression of rural education also became embedded in the mindset of interview participants.

Second, deficit thinking can be identified in EGRT's mainstream media advocacy and content of its official website. Children are represented as attentive and enthusiastic, eager to learn, implying that the only problem that these children face is that they are deprived of quality education by the accident of birth into a place of poverty, subject to unequal and unjustifiable structural conditions. The teacher is presented as the crucial factor of quality education, the 'superman' or 'superwoman' who can transform this situation with their talent and commitment. This strategy creates the illusion that teacher efforts could save children from systemic inequality.

The marketing discourse of EGRT made it hard for participants to see the real but hidden social factors which had already put local students and teachers in a disadvantaged position. Therefore, EGRT applicants might be seduced into thinking that they could fix the problems of low achieving students through their personal efforts as teachers. The interview participants, including Feng, Shuang, Ren, Hua and Wei, commented that they had been deeply moved when they saw the pictures and video materials on the EGRT official website. It was due in part to these moving pictures and videos that they had decided to join EGRT (Yin, 2018). They tended to project the images of students featured in the promotional materials onto their own future students.

Third, deficit thinking may also stem from the unequal distribution of prosperity produced by the rapid economic growth of the past 30 years. An urban-rural divide and massive income gap appears to generate social contempt towards rurality by classifying rural people as backward and inferior (Li, 2013). This attitude was reflected in the responses of EGRT fellows who tended to classify rural areas and rural education as inferior. None mentioned their students' particular cultures, values, or traditions. Thus, these prestigious university graduates seem to represent a superior urban population, who are the normal and able central group, while the rural population become abnormal and less able 'others' (Bourdieu & Wacquant, 1992). Following Bourdieu and Wacquant (1992), this process might show that the classification schemas of habitus are not simply imposed on the larger population by dominant groups. Rather, they are naturalised and taken for granted, (mis)recognised as legitimate by the dominant groups, and gradually become social consensus. The EGRT fellows' experience demonstrates how the classification schemas of habitus work through the judgements of others with a set of distinctive signs. Thus, by virtue of their classification schemas of habitus, the interview participants made judgements about local education (Bourdieu, 1988).

More specifically, the classification schemata of habitus worked to generate a deficit discourse among interview participants regardless of their urban or rural origin. As shown previously in Table 3.1, many interview participants (12 of 14) had graduated from the most prestigious universities of China, and almost every one (13 of 14) had received secondary education in local key schools. Therefore, they could be regarded as "winners" throughout their careers in the current educational system; and most of them seemed to have become used to their superior positions amongst their peers. Thus, they could be understood to have rich cultural capital, symbolic capital, and even economic capital if they came from affluent families.

The six interview participants with rural origins tended to share the same deficit discourse with their urban counterparts. Their values and views appeared to have been produced and internalised through exposure to a privileged culture. This finding seems to mirror Australian research showing that the success of "wonder students" within the education system is "dependent, at least in part, on abandoning their own working-class background" (Lampert, Burnett, & Lebhers, 2016, p. 38).

In summary, the interview participants seem to display mental schemata that are the embodiment of social division, "structurally homologous" and "genetically linked" (Bourdieu & Wacquant, 1992, p. 13). Cumulative exposure to certain social conditions (e.g., social media, EGRT advertisement strategies, rural-urban gap) seemed to have instilled in these individuals an ensemble of durable and transferable dispositions that have internalized the external social environment (Bourdieu & Wacquant, 1992). This becomes manifest in the deficit discourse they apply to students in disadvantaged rural schools.

Conclusion and Implication

Through a sociological lens, this chapter has explored the experience of 14 fellows of an alternative teacher training and employment program in China.

This exploration of the EGRT fellows' experience indicates the complexity of the transitioning experience of graduates from prestigious universities to disadvantaged rural schools. It has revealed significant disparities between the fellows' expectations and perceived impact on their students' education. These disparities were apparently influenced by pervasive deficit discourse about social conditions and inhabitants of rural communities, especially in the EGRT marketing, recruitment, and training materials. The deficit discourse can compound educational disadvantage, by adversely affecting the fellows' teaching approach and relationships with their students and local teachers.

For the fellows, their gradual realisation of the disparities often generated negative emotional responses, with potential risk to their teaching practice and wellbeing. This risk warrants further investigation. The findings suggest a need for alternative teacher training organisations in China to more accurately represent the social conditions that fellows are likely to encounter when on service, and to more rigorously prepare them for the challenges of teaching in an unfamiliar field of relative disadvantage. This recommendation applies to recruitment processes and materials, and to pre- and in-service training programs, all of which could be enhanced by deeper sociological understanding.

Note

1. Exceptional Graduates as Rural Teachers (EGRT) is a pseudonym adopted for an alternative teaching program in China that was the context of this research. The graduate teacher participants are referred to as fellows.

References

Anderson, A. (2013). Teach For America and symbolic violence: A Bourdieuian analysis of education's next quick-fix. *The Urban Review*, *45*(5), 684–700.

Bourdieu, P. (1977). *Outline of a theory of practice*. Cambridge: Cambridge University Press.

Bourdieu, P. (1983). The field of cultural production, or: The economic world reversed. *Poetics*, *12*(4–5), 311–356.

Bourdieu, P. (1984). *Distinction: A Social Critique of the Judgement of Taste*. Cambridge, Mass: Harvard University Press.

Bourdieu, P. (1986). The forms of capital. In J. G. Richardson (Ed.), *Handbook of theory and research for the sociology of education*. Westport, CT: Greenwood Press.

Bourdieu, P. (1990). *In other words: Essays towards a reflexive sociology*. Stanford, CA: Stanford University Press.

Bourdieu, P. (1993). *Sociology in question*. London: Sage.

Bourdieu, P. (1988). *Homo academicus*. Newbury Park, CA: Stanford University Press.

Bourdieu, P. & Wacquant, L. (1992). *An invitation to reflexive sociology.* Chicago & London: The University of Chicago Press.

Boyd, D., Lankford, H., Loeb, S., & Wyckoff, J. (2005). Explaining the short careers of high-achieving teachers in schools with low-performing students. *American economic review, 95*(2), 166–171.

Braun, V., & Clarke, V. (2006). Using thematic analysis in psychology. *Qualitative Research in Psychology, 3*(2), 77–101.

Brewer, T. J. (2014). Accelerated burnout: How Teach For America's academic impact model and theoretical culture of accountability can foster disillusionment among its corps members. *Educational Studies, 50*(3), 246–263.

Crawford-Garrett, K. (2017). "The problem is bigger than us": Grappling with educational inequity in Teach First New Zealand. *Teaching and Teacher Education, 68,* 91–98.

Dooley, K., Exley, B., & Poulus, D. (2016). Research on critical EFL literacies: An illustrative analysis of some college level programs in Taiwan. *English Teaching & Learning [英语教学], 40*(4), 39–64.

Holloway, I., & Todres, L. (2003). The status of method: Flexibility, consistency and coherence. *Qualitative Research, 3*(3), 345–357.

Ingersoll, R. M. (2003). The teacher shortage: Myth or reality? *Educational Horizons, 81*(3), 146–152.

La Londe, P. G., Brewer, T. J., & Lubienski, C. A. (2015). Teach For America and Teach For All: Creating an intermediary organization network for global education reform. *Education Policy Analysis Archives, 23*(47), 1–28.

Lam, S. G. (2017). *Teach for America goes to China: Teach for China, educational equity, and public sphere participation in education* (Doctor of Philosophy), University of Wisconsin-Madison, Madison.

Lampert, J., Burnett, B., & Davie, S. (2012). Preparing high achieving English teachers to work in disadvantaged schools: 'I'll teach Shakespeare when I'm 60.' *English in Australia, 47*(3), 69.

Lampert, J., Burnett, B., & Lebhers, S. (2016). 'More like the kids than the other teachers': One working-class pre-service Teacher's experiences in a middle-class profession. *Teaching and Teacher Education, 58,* 35–42.

Li, H. (2013). Rural students' experiences in a Chinese elite university: Capital, habitus and practices. *British Journal of Sociology of Education, 34*(5–6), 829–847.

Lin, J.-H. (2012). *Coming to belong: A narrative analysis of international students' experience in an Australian university.* (Doctor of Philosophy), Queensland University of Technology, Brisbane.

Marom, N. (2014). Planning as a principle of vision and division: A Bourdieusian view of Tel Aviv's urban development, 1920s–1950s. *Environment and Planning A, 46*(8), 1908–1926.

McCann, T. M., Johannessen, L. R., & Ricca, B. (2005). Responding to new teachers' Concerns. *Educational Leadership, 62*(8), 30–34.

Muijs, D., Chapman, C., & Armstrong, P. (2013). Can early careers teachers be teacher leaders? A study of second-year trainees in the teach first alternative certification programme. *Educational Management Administration & Leadership, 41*(6), 767–781.

Olmedo, A., Bailey, P. L., & Ball, S. J. (2013). To infinity and beyond . . .: Heterarchical governance, the Teach For All network in Europe and the making of profits and minds. *European Educational Research Journal, 12*(4), 492–512.

Rao, J., & Ye, J. (2016). From a virtuous cycle of rural-urban education to urban-oriented rural basic education in China: An explanation of the failure of China's Rural School Mapping Adjustment policy. *Journal of Rural Studies, 47*, 601–611.

Schaffer, C. L., White, M., & Brown, C. M. (2016). *Questioning assumptions and challenging perceptions: Becoming an effective teacher in urban environments.* Lanham, MD: Rowman & Littlefield.

Skourdoumbis, A. (2012). Teach for Australia (TFA): Can it overcome educational disadvantage? *Asia Pacific Journal of Education, 32*(3), 305–315.

Smart, S., Hutchings, M., Maylor, U., Mendick, H., & Menter, I. (2009). Processes of middle-class reproduction in a graduate employment scheme. *Journal of Education and Work, 22*(1), 35–53.

Straubhaar, R., & Gottfried, M. (2016). Who joins Teach for America and why? Insights into the "typical" recruit in an urban school district. *Education and Urban Society, 48*(7), 627–649.

Tamir, E. (2009). Choosing to teach in urban schools among graduates of elite colleges. *Urban Education, 44*(5), 522–544.

Yin, Y. (2018). *From prestigious university to teachers in disadvantaged schools: A sociological study of participation in an alternative teacher recruitment program.* (Doctor of Philosophy), Queensland University of Technology, Brisbane.

Yin, Y., Dooley, K., & Mu, G. (2019). Educational practice in a field of mediation: Elite university graduates' participation experience of an alternative program of school-teacher recruitment for rural China. In G. Mu, K. Dooley, & A. Luke (Eds.), *Bourdieu and Chinese education: Inequality, competition, and change* (pp. 81–96). New York: Routledge.

Yiu, L., & Adams, J. (2013). Reforming rural education in China: Understanding teacher expectations for rural youth. *The China Quarterly, 216*, 993–1017.

Zhou, H., & Shang, X. (2011). Short-term volunteer teachers in rural China: Challenges and needs. *Frontiers of Education in China, 6*(4), 571–601.

4. *Teach First Ask Questions Later: Experiencing a Policy Entrepreneur in New Zealand*

SAM OLDHAM
New Zealand

Biosketch

Sam Oldham is a PhD candidate at the University of Melbourne. His research is broadly concerned with education governance and curriculum, new policy actors, and aspects of the relationship between education systems and the economic domain. He has taught English and Social Science at public schools throughout Australia and New Zealand.

Narrative

Teach First New Zealand (TFNZ) is a relatively new addition to the Teach For All (TFAll) network. Founded in 2011 by Shaun Sutton, a Teach First (U.K.) graduate, TFNZ is the model policy entrepreneur, embodying an eagerness for change, a penchant for innovation, and a willingness to take risks in pursuit of its aims (Mintrom, 2000). Previously confined to high-poverty areas of South Auckland and Northland, TFNZ candidates are available to schools throughout the country as of 2019, with the organisation doubling the size of its annual cohort to 80. I began with TFNZ for the 2015 school year. On a personal level, I loved my two years on the program. Despite the challenges of TFNZ (often referred to as the "TFNZ scheme"), it introduced me to teaching, as well as to countless incredible people, many of whom I am grateful to have known. Among them are the hundreds of young people who have passed through my classrooms over the years. It is for these young people and others like them, however, that I am now compelled to oppose TFNZ in the strongest terms. TFNZ, I believe, stands to do immeasurable harm to education in Aotearoa New Zealand. Indeed, it commits harm every day—by appointing unqualified, inexperienced trainees to low-income schools, TFNZ deprives students in those schools of their right to a qualified teacher. The organization imposes upon low-income students a burden that their middle and upper-income peers do not share. Due to enduring legacies of racism and colonialism, this burden is carried overwhelmingly by Māori and Pasifika students who, through no fault or choice of their own, find themselves participating in someone else's training.

In this chapter, I reflect on my experiences in TFNZ to shed light on certain aspects of the program. In the following section, I discuss the process by which I came to be opposed to TFNZ, with particular reference to the power of the organisation's marketing and communications. At times, I have wondered why the facts above are not more obvious to people. I have wondered, for example, why TFNZ is not challenged more often on its claim that it is combatting inequality. When I reflect on my own experience, however, I have to acknowledge that it took me months to properly understand TFNZ, even when the basic facts of it were staring me in the face. Looking back, I believe my early inability to fully understand TFNZ had a lot to do with the sophistication of its marketing, communications, and specific aspects its training—what together might simply be called "spin"—directed at both the public and its own participants. Developing a clear understanding of TFNZ beyond the spin is, I believe, crucial for anyone concerned with fairness and equity in education in Aotearoa New Zealand. In subsequent sections, I discuss an employment relations dispute between TFNZ and the secondary teachers' union, the Post-Primary Teachers' Association (PPTA). In late 2015, TFNZ was found to be in breach of employment law and, as a result, participants were at risk of losing their teaching positions. As a TFNZ participant and a delegate for the PPTA, I observed what I perceived to be a degree of irresponsibility on behalf of TFNZ. Above all, TFNZ seemed to display a willingness to privilege its own survival over the interests of students and teachers. Finally, I discuss the experience of criticising TFNZ in the public domain, reflecting on the "activist" nature of the organisation, and its broader implications for education policy.

Life in the Fast Track: Separating Spin From Reality

Perhaps what strikes me most about TFNZ is the gulf between what it claims to be and the reality of what it is. There is something almost Orwellian about a program that claims to reduce educational inequality by putting the best teachers in front of low-income students, while arguably doing the complete opposite. Precisely *how* this has been allowed to happen, I believe, has much to do with TFNZ's ability to sell itself to the education sector and the public. This occurs through its marketing, for which it has won awards, but also its communications with participants and other stakeholders. If it is not already evident, it is my strong suspicion that the work of protecting and advancing TFAll in this way is collaborative within the global network—that the various affiliates assist each other in developing communications strategies and materials. By the time TFNZ was established in 2011, it had more than 20 years of knowledge and resources from its international network to draw on.

My first meaningful experience of the gap between TFNZ spin and reality was in trying to make sense of the scheme during my first weeks on the Summer Initial Intensive. I was elated upon being accepted to the program. I had a background in student activism, including serving as a founding member of a national organisation for free tertiary education and a paid organiser for my university student union. I had spent years working as a teaching assistant in public schools throughout New Zealand and Australia, including at an alternative education program for students exited from schools in low-income areas. Despite these experiences (or perhaps because of them), I struggled to understand or articulate the mission of the organisation with which I was now affiliated. In seminars, we were taught that our mission was to mitigate a problem called "educational inequality," but I had no idea how inexperienced, trainee teachers were supposed to do that, and the phenomenon of educational inequality itself, despite TFNZ's efforts, made limited sense to me. When I spoke to people outside of TFNZ, they likewise struggled. When I told a friend that it was intended to promote equality by lifting outcomes for students in low-income schools, she responded: "but *how*, when you're still training?" The significance of these sorts of responses was not lost on me.

It was made clear to us, directly and indirectly, that TFNZ recruited elite trainees, but this only left me with more questions. Some in my cohort (and others we worked with) had postgraduate degrees and experience teaching English abroad or university tutoring. Some had been established in other professions. A tiny handful of us had any background in activism, and I was one of very few with experience working in schools. Many of the people in my cohort were fascinating and inspiring people, but I failed to see how we differed so significantly from other teachers aside from credentialing and formal training, and I include myself in this assessment. Around 15% of my cohort left before the end of the two years, and some of these people were completely unsuited to teaching despite having made it through the selection process. Above all, I could not then (and cannot now) understand why strong academic results and personal achievement should, for some people, be substitutes for initial teacher education (ITE).

Of course, it is impossible to debate fully the efficacy of TFNZ's selection process because the organisation conceals its details (beyond a set of broad criteria available via its website). This is true of other TFAll affiliates, such as Teach For America (Brewer, 2013). It is my belief that this is necessary because the selection criteria are not as rigorous as the organisation suggests. At my Assessment Centre, I was asked to participate in a brief group exercise (a mock staff meeting), deliver a 10-minute "lesson" to TFNZ staff, and participate in an interview (a process that is virtually identical to the Teach For America selection process). The "leadership qualities" by which candidates are apparently selected still elude me. Someone associated with the scheme tells me, with approbation, that a recent recruit participated in a popular television show. The implication here is deeply problematic: if you have done something sufficiently dazzling, you can take the fast-track to low-income classrooms. TFNZ emphasises that it selects people who are genuinely concerned with equality in education and beyond. It has to be said: when there is a scholarship and a two-year salaried position on the line, people will inevitably lie about this. On the TFNZ website you can take a quiz to assess how "well aligned" you are with the program, with questions on a scale of 1 to 10 such as, "How much do you care about the issue of educational inequality in Aotearoa New Zealand?" Or how likely are you to give away your "takeaway curry" to a homeless person? (Teach First NZ, 2018a). This absurdly low bar for commitment makes a mockery of social change.

At some point during my two years with the scheme, I realised that the initial training had not properly prepared me for teaching—that I did not simply *feel* out my depth, as TFNZ staff suggested, but that I was. TFNZ training stressed that we were doing fine and that we should have confidence in our abilities. We were reminded that we had passed through a highly-tuned selection process and, despite lacking the formal education training of our public sector counterparts, were well-prepared. We were told that it was normal for participants to fail and to feel inadequate. We were indeed *encouraged* to fail as part of the learning process: "fail early, fail often" was a mantra that we shared. We were told that, because we were high-achievers, we were simply not used to failure and should not be so hard on ourselves. Of course, left unsaid was the fact that our students would also suffer through this process of their teachers "learning through failure." Our failures in the classroom were also our students' failures, observed through disengagement, dissatisfaction, test scores, and so on. These were the ways that "we" failed. We were also presented with the idea—and many of us perpetuated it—that graduate teachers from traditional ITE also felt inadequate, or even *were* inadequate. Of course, the purpose of any ITE program should be to have graduates *as prepared as possible* for teaching, rather than comparing degrees of unpreparedness.

TFNZ bitterly rejects the criticism that it is a fast-track scheme, and much of its spin seeks to obscure this fact. To skirt the obviously fast-tracked nature of the program, TFNZ emphasises its two-year duration. Of course, when it is thought of as a two-year program, then, compared with New Zealand's one-year postgraduate teaching diploma, it is not a fast track. It is undeniably, however, a fast track to the classroom. No other ITE program allows teachers to be responsible for classes in schools after six-to-eight weeks of seminars. At times, the organisation has been flatly disingenuous on the issue. In a 2016 Select Committee submission (see section below), TFNZ allegedly described its participants as "unsupervised at times" within their schools (Jones, 2016). This is a flagrant distortion—TFNZ participants are appointed with all the classroom responsibilities of a teacher, observed occasionally by a school-based mentor or TFNZ staff member for the purposes of training or assessment. TFNZ spin was also directed at participants on this issue. As part of the initial intensive, TFNZ gave us training in "how to talk about Teach First." Despite assuring us that it was "not brainwashing", we were taught how to respond to criticisms of the organisation, including how to defend against the idea that it was a fast-track alternative. In short, we were reminded that the scheme took two years to complete. I felt deeply uncomfortable with this particular seminar, especially given that another of the canned defences it offered was against the idea that it was promoting "corporate reform" to education.

I believe my experience in coming to a clear understanding of TFNZ is instructive. Quite simply, the scheme does not make sense—inexperienced trainees are in no position to provide quality teaching. And there are no personal qualities or academic achievements that can replace a robust and comprehensive ITE. What's more, if it is true that some teachers are better prepared for employment-based training than others, to have the matter determined by a charity with limited public oversight is, in my opinion, indefensible. I was naïve in joining TFNZ, though I do believe the TFAll model can be difficult to understand for people who have not been in teaching, or perhaps even through the model itself. Developing shared understanding will be important to building opposition.

The Outlaw Trainees: Employment Legislation and School Appointments

During my time in the program, a longstanding dispute between TFNZ and the PPTA came to a head. This dispute may be insightful in the broad context of TFAll. In some ways, it seemed to reflect TFNZ proponents' desire to implement a predetermined organisational model and to bend the local context to fit. Former PPTA President, Angela Roberts, stresses that the dispute occurred in part due to a failure by TFNZ executives and others to accept that state sector employment law in New Zealand differed from that in the U.K. (Moir, 2015). In the words of New Zealand's Employment Relations Authority (ERA), "the effect of the Teach First arrangements are to seek to abrogate the usual rules by purporting to create a new class of employee which somehow avoids the effect of the collective agreement and the relevant statute law" (Determination of ERA, 2015, p. 12). Despite TFNZ's emphasis on its independent, local nature, the employment dispute seemed to suggest that it came pre-packaged, closer perhaps to a sort of franchise. As part of this, some aspects of the dispute point to a certain recklessness in the behaviour of people responsible for TFNZ executives, including privileging the future of their organisation over the interests of participants and schools.

In November 2015, the ERA ruled that TFNZ's process of appointing participants to schools was in breach of the State Sector Act and the Secondary Teachers Collective Agreement. In short, TFNZ had been insisting that its participants were not teachers, but were trainees occupying specially created training positions within schools. As such, these positions did not need to be advertised and could simply be filled through agreement between TFNZ and schools. The PPTA's position was that TFNZ participants *were* indeed teachers and that their positions needed to be advertised so that qualified teachers could also apply (Determination of ERA, 2015). In November 2015, the ERA ruled in favour of the PPTA. For a period of several months, there was uncertainty about what the outcome of the dispute would be, and even the security of TFNZ participants' teaching contracts. The dispute was resolved in March 2016 when TFNZ "agreed that Teach First NZ participants will now apply and be considered for jobs in schools alongside other teachers" (Ministry of Education, 2016). Despite press reports that our schools would be "left with nobody to put in front of classes" (Moir, 2015), existing TFNZ participants were able to continue teaching unaffected.

It is likely that TFNZ had always suspected, if not known outright, that its appointment process was illegal. The ERA ruling was categorical: it was "difficult to escape the conclusion" that a TFNZ participant was a teacher like any other for the purposes of employment law (Determination of ERA, 2015, p. 7). In forceful terms, the Determination "refused to accept [...] there is a sort of new category of Teach First position within the education sector. That is certainly a manufactured reality" (Determination of ERA, 2015, p. 11). Moreover, the PPTA had insisted that TFNZ was in breach of the law more or less since the program's inception (Moir, 2015). TFNZ (with support from the Minister of Education) consistently denied that it was at fault, resulting in the legal dispute. It is my feeling that, rather than face an existential threat so early in its life, TFNZ decided to ignore warnings about its appointment process until it was better established and in a better position to confront the problem. Indeed, this was exactly how the dispute unfolded. It seems fair to assume that TFNZ was at least aware of the possibility that its practices were illegal, which reflects poorly on the organisation's decision to proceed as normal, recruiting successive cohorts on shaky foundations.

TFNZ may have weathered the tempest unscathed, but the impact of the dispute was still significant. The program had to be restructured at the last minute for the incoming cohort, forcing these participants to take a significant pay cut or leave the program. For months there was lingering uncertainty about my cohort's future. Sensationalist media reports claimed that we might lose our jobs at any moment, a claim that was picked up and circulated by members of the public who knew of the case. Despite TFNZ's assurances to its participants, no party to the dispute knew what orders the ERA might give. In my own communications with the ERA, I was told that our schools might be fined for breaching employment law. Staff within my school implied that our positions might be terminated. At one point, the idea that we might be encouraged to *take our schools to court* if they tried to terminate our employment agreements was circulated. Regardless of what may have been the outcome, a recklessness on behalf of TFNZ was undeniable.

Other facts of the dispute seem to reflect poorly on TFNZ. To end it, TFNZ agreed that its participants would in the future compete for advertised job openings alongside qualified teachers. Within weeks, the organisation was supporting proposed legislation that would allow its participants to once again have access to unadvertised teaching positions. I strongly suspect that TFNZ representatives even helped to initiate this reform (in the form a Supplementary Order). By that stage, the organisation had the support of then Minister of Education, Hekia Parata, and I doubt that Parata herself would have acted so quickly and enthusiastically without TFNZ encouragement. Either way, TFNZ made the only submission to support the legislation during the Select Committee process (Education Legislation Bill, 2016). One is ultimately left wondering: if TFNZ candidates are so capable, why has the organisation done everything to protect them from competition with regular teachers?

TFNZ has often promoted itself as lifting the status of the teaching profession. In one op-ed, TFNZ's former CEO declared (rightly) that "we should be aiming for the day when becoming a teacher is as competitive and prestigious as it is to become a doctor, lawyer, or engineer" (Sutton, 2016). In its communications with the ERA, however, attempts by TFNZ to blur the definition of a teacher seem to contradict this objective. To support its argument that its participants should not be considered teachers for the purposes of employment law, TFNZ proposed that "there is no clear definition of either a teacher or a teaching position because [...] there are a variety of definitions offered across a range of statutes" (Determination of ERA, 2015). The ERA response was firm: "we understand a teacher to be a person who instructs students" (Determination of ERA, 2015). It seems odd that an organisation committed to lifting the status of teachers would suggest that there is no real definition of one. The President of the early childhood and primary teachers' union, Lynda Stuart, offers (in a different context) a poignant response: "We don't debate the titles of doctor or lawyer, so I think the time for ensuring we are really careful around the use of the word teacher is here" (Hancock & Cowlishore, 2018). This might be considered a specific example of TFNZ engaging in deprofessionalisation while, once again, marketing itself as doing the complete opposite.

Teach First, Ask Questions Later

Since leaving TFNZ, I have been vocal in my opposition to the scheme in the media and elsewhere (Oldham, 2017, 2018). As a result, I have sometimes faced bitter reactions from former and current participants. There is no denying that an "all together" attitude prevails within the organisation. To some degree, this is institutional. Participants are expected to support TFNZ's mission if they are even to be selected. Such attitudes are further encouraged by marketing and through the seminars, through the "we're-in-this-together" attitudes of coordinators and other participants, and by other means. At best, this produces a strange hybrid between an activist organisation and a training programme. At worst, it leads to the "cultishness" that TFAll affiliates are sometimes described as possessing. Indeed, "cult" was a term sometimes thrown around by my cohort. In my first conversation with a Teach For Australia representative, she described her organisation warmly as a "like a cult" and I was welcomed to "the movement." The term "movement" has been often used by Teach For America (Winn, 2012; Teach For America, 2019).

I believe that this feature of the organisation does have serious implications. Above all, an ITE program, perhaps *any* education program, should maintain a clear organisational boundary between students and coordinators, or between students and the program itself. This allows room for meaningful dissent and disagreement—I did not feel confident to express my opposition to TFNZ while I was in the scheme, as I wondered (and wonder still) to what extent they were empowered to simply dump me. This differs strongly from a traditional university program. More importantly, clear boundaries ensure proper degrees of organisational responsibility. During the employment dispute, for example, I felt particularly frustrated by the use of inclusive language by TFNZ coordinators to the effect that "we would all get through it", and so on. The facts were clear to me: there were those responsible for the governance of the organisation (executives, board members, and so on) and there were participants. The former had culpability for the dispute; the latter did not. Both, however, were being expected to deal with the consequences. In my opinion, this an unusual and unhealthy organisational dynamic, and one that poses risks for participants.

Perhaps a more significant consequence is that, as part of the political goals of the organisation, participants are given a narrow and problematic view of educational inequality. Internationally, research shows that educational inequality is overwhelmingly an outcome of socioeconomic inequality (Benn & Millar, 2006; Carpenter & Osborne, 2014; Fergusson, Horwood & Boden, 2008; Harker, 1995; OECD, 2013; Wylie, 2011, 2012). The most comprehensive examination of the relationship in New Zealand draws the conclusion that, in trying to mitigate educational inequality,

> schools have been, and remain, relatively powerless. Closing the gap requires a more holistic emphasis on policies to remove the causes and consequences of poverty and other social inequalities that affect the likelihood of educational success. According to this research, it is clearly unfair and unreasonable to hold schools and teachers accountable for the differences in attainment of social groups, most of which are outside their control. (Snook & O'Neill, 2014, p. 25)

To attempt to mitigate educational inequality through teaching, though it may feel heroic, is a misuse of energy and resources and a distortion of the real issue. It leads inevitably to blaming teachers and schools for problems that are beyond the control of both. Consider TFNZ's summary of the issue on its website: "In Aotearoa New Zealand, thousands of Kiwi kids are falling through the cracks of our education system each year [...] While our education system is working well for many, thousands of students leave school every year without the most basic qualification" (Teach First NZ, 2018b). The point here is clear: educational inequality is a problem of the *education system*, not the economy and society, perpetuating a myth that creates the "need" for organizations like TFNZ. While improved responsiveness to Māori and Pasifika students in schools remains a critical space for action in Aotearoa, TFNZ has not articulated how it intends to address this issue in ways that would shift the dial on unequal achievement, or even in ways that differ significantly from their traditionally-certificated peers. Rather, as mentioned above, it is my feeling that TFNZ actually *contributes* to inequities for

Māori and Pasifika young people who make up the overwhelming majority of student cohorts served by TFNZ trainees. In recent years, the relationship between inequality and education in New Zealand has become a topic of national conversation (see, for example, Clark, 2015; Johnston, 2015, 2016, 2018; *National Business Review*, 2017; Parata, 2015). As TFNZ increases in size and more of its alumni move into leadership and policy positions, the organisation's problematic conception of the issue may become a thorn in the side of progressive reform efforts.

Another point must be made here. Where teaching salaries are low, TFAll actors are more likely to thrive. In Aotearoa New Zealand, where schools are in the grip of a national staffing crisis, it may be harder to generate support for the scheme's cancellation. TFNZ does hold water on one point: a trainee teacher is better than no teacher at all. In Aotearoa, as elsewhere, major increases to teachers' salaries are needed to attract and retain people in teaching. However, there are other alternatives. The TeachNZ scheme, which pays thousands of dollars in grants to qualified teachers who begin and remain in low-income schools, represents a genuine example of equity-based policy. Bali Haque, a prominent education reform advocate, promotes salary loading for teachers in low-income schools (Haque, 2014). In New Zealand, where teacher pay is standardised nationally, there is less incentive for teachers to work in low-income schools where challenges of workload can be much greater, or to live in expensive urban centres such as Auckland at all. Some defensible version of employment-based teacher training might someday exist in New Zealand, and successful international examples might be considered. But putting employment-based trainees exclusively in low-income schools is indefensible. Above all, policy around ITE should be considered in relation to the principle that every student is entitled to a qualified teacher. Programs should be subjected to the highest levels of public input, oversight, transparency, and accountability. Those that fail by these standards should not be spared the axe.

References

Benn, M. & Millar, F. (2006). *A Comprehensive Future: Quality and Equality for all our Children*. London, UK: Compass.

Brewer, T. J. (2013). From the Trenches: A Teach for America Corp Member's Perspective. *Critical Education*, 4(12), 1–17. Retrieved October 1, 2019 from http://ojs.library.ubc.ca/index.php/criticaled/article/view/183939

Carpenter, V. & Osborne, S. (2014). *Twelve Thousand Hours: Education and Poverty in Aotearoa New Zealand*. Auckland: Dunmore Publishing.

Clark, J. (16 November 2015). The inequality of school achievement. *New Zealand Herald*. Retrieved October 1, 2019 from https://www.nzherald.co.nz/nz/news/article.cfm?c_id=1&objectid=11546091

Determination of the New Zealand Employment Relations Authority: New Zealand Post-Primary Teachers' Association vs. Secretary for Education, University of Auckland, Teach First New Zealand Trust. (27 November 2015).

Education Legislation Bill (August 2016). First Reading. Retrieved October 1, 2019 from https://www.parliament.nz/en/pb/hansard-debates/rhr/combined/HansDeb_20160816_20160816_28

Fergusson, D. M., Horwood, L. J. & Boden, J. M. (2008). The transmission of social inequality: Examination of the linkages between family socioeconomic status in childhood and educational achievement in young adulthood. *Research in Social Stratification and Mobility*, 26, pp. 277–295.

Hancock, F. & Cowlishaw, S. (April 6, 2018). Lift in Teacher Status Could Breach Bill of Rights. *Newsroom* (online). Retrieved October 1, 2019 from https://www.newsroom.co.nz/2018/04/05/102736/protecting-the-title-of-teacher-could-breach-the-bill-of-rights

Haque, B. (2014). *Changing Our Secondary Schools*. Wellington: NZCER Press.

Harker, R. (1995). Further comment on "do schools matter?" *New Zealand Journal of Educational Studies*, 30(1), pp. 73–76.

Johnston, K. (4 November 2015). Education Investigation: The Great Divide. *New Zealand Herald* (online). Retrieved October 1, 2019 from https://www.nzherald.co.nz/nz/news/article.cfm?c_id=1&objectid=11539592

Johnston, K. (15 September 2018). Want to be a doctor, lawyer, or engineer? Don't grow up poor. *New Zealand Herald* (online). Retrieved October 1, 2019 from https://www.nzherald.co.nz/nz/news/article.cfm?c_id=1&objectid=12123299

Jones, N. (14 June 2016). Law change for Teach First attacked. *New Zealand Herald* (online). Retrieved October 1, 2019 from https://www.nzherald.co.nz/nz/news/article.cfm?c_id=1&objectid=11656202

Ministry of Education (18 March 2016). Media Statement: Agreement on Future Employment Processes involving Teach First NZ. Retrieved October 1, 2019 from https://www.ppta.org.nz/advice-and-issues/fast-track-teacher-education-programmes-teach-first-nz/

Mintrom, M. (2000). *Policy entrepreneurs and school choice*. Georgetown University Press: Washington, D.C.

Moir, J. (6 December 2015). Authority rules top teachers illegal to alarm of schools left with nobody to put in front of classes. *Stuff* (online). Retrieved October 1, 2019 from https://www.stuff.co.nz/national/education/74730951/Authority-rules-top-teachers-trainees-illegal-to-alarm-of-schools-left-with-nobody-to-put-in-front-of-classes

National Business Review (17 February 2017). NZ's unequal education system. *National Business Review* (online). Retrieved October 1, 2019 from https://www.nbr.co.nz/opinion/nz-politics-daily-nz%E2%80%99s-unequal-education-system

OECD. (2013). 2012: PISA results: Excellence Through Equity (Volume 11). Giving Every student the chance to succeed. Paris, France: OECD.

Oldham, S. (2017). Opinion: Putting Graduates into Classrooms Does Not Always Work. *New Zealand Herald*. Retrieved October 1, 2019 from http://www.nzherald.co.nz/nz/news/article.cfm?c_id=1&objectid=11958320

Oldham, S. (2018). Teach First NZ expanding at student expense. EducationCentral.co.nz. Retrieved October 1, 2019 from https://educationcentral.co.nz/opinion-sam-oldham-teach-first-nz-expanding-at-student-expense/

Parata, H. (6 November 2015). Socioeconomic factors are often overstated. *New Zealand Herald* (online). Retrieved October 1, 2019 from https://www.nzherald.co.nz/opinion/news/article.cfm?c_id=466&objectid=11540766

Snook, I & O'Neill, J. Poverty and Inequality of Educational Achievement. In Carpenter, V. & Osborne, S. (2014). *Twelve Thousand Hours: Education and Poverty in Aotearoa New Zealand*. Auckland, NZ: Dunmore.

Sutton, S. (11 May 2016). Shaun Sutton: teaching, where only the best will do. *New Zealand Herald* (online). Retrieved October 1, 2019 from https://www.nzherald.co.nz/nz/news/article.cfm?c_id=1&objectid=11636872

Teach First NZ (2018a). *Teach First: What will you lead next?* Retrieved October 1, 2019 from https://quiz.weirdlyhub.com/quiz/teachfirstnz/teach-first-what-will-you-lead-next

Teach First NZ (2018b). What's the issue? Retrieved October 1, 2019 from https://teachfirstnz.org/programme/whats-the-issue

Teach for America (2019). Our History. Retrieved October 14, 2019 from https://www.teachforamerica.org/what-we-do/history

Wylie, C. (2013). Schools and Inequality. In Rashbrooke, M. (Ed.) *Inequality: A New Zealand Crisis*. (pp. 134–144). Wellington: Bridget Williams Books.

Winn, R. (17 July 2012). How to Start the Movement. *TeacherPop* (Teach for America). Retrieved October 1, 2019 from https://www.teachforamerica.org/teacherpop/how-start-movement

Section II Leadership Cultivation Over Teaching

5. Leaders in the Community or Educators in the Classroom? Problematic Dual Roles of Fellows at Teach For China

SARA G. LAM, TONGJI PHILIP QIAN, AND FAN ADA WANG
China

Biosketch

Sara G. Lam is an assistant professor of education at the University of Minnesota, Morris. Her teaching and research focuses on educational equity and democratic participation in education in rural areas of China and the U.S. She is a co-founder and board member of the Rural China Education Foundation. Previously, she has taught and provided in-service teacher professional development in rural China.

Tongji Philip Qian is a visual artist and the founder of TPQ Studio. His current artistic practice attempts to locate limits of his ego and physicality through works on paper, whereas his writings on teaching and art criticism intentionally resist such personal moments and focus on students, institutions, context, and variation. Qian is currently an MFA candidate at Rhode Island School of Design, and he lives and works in both Providence and New York City.

Fan Ada Wang is the founder of Wei Shai Studio in Shanghai where she produces naturally-dyed textiles and hosts educational workshops. Her interest in craftsmanship stems from years of teaching in rural areas in China and in India, and she believes teaching can exist and have greater potential outside the limits of contemporary institutions. Wang is currently an MA candidate in International and Comparative Education at Teachers College, focusing on family and community education.

Narrative

Teach For China (TFC), like all Teach For All (TFAll) affiliates, aims to not only provide outstanding teachers to schools that are under-resourced but also develop and support education reform leaders. One way TFC cultivates teaching fellows' (TFC teachers) leadership is by encouraging them to initiate projects beyond their regular classroom teaching responsibilities that will bring positive impact to local communities. As new teachers and newcomers to rural communities, TFC fellows are expected to achieve excellence as teachers and to lead projects for community change. This chapter explores the relationship between these dual goals based on one fellow-led project, *Community Ownership, Rediscovery and Engagement* (CORE), which was initiated by fellows in the Heqing County in 2011 with the purpose of providing a guided extracurricular program for students to learn research and communication skills from exploring the immediate local community. We are interested in CORE as the center of our research because it is often held up as an exemplar of fellows' community impact. For this chapter, we intend to attempt a different format: we hope to offer readers an eclectic perspective on CORE projects with lenses of a TFC fellow who directly participated in CORE, a fellow who did not conduct any community projects, and a rural education researcher. Therefore, we collaborated to write the introduction, but we independently composed our mini-chapters with our own conclusions. We feel that an overarching culmination for the whole chapter will only limit the open-ended nature of this three-way exchange on education. We hope that with our creative presentation, readers will be able to reflect on, to contextualize, and to question our writings.

Born and raised in Beijing, Fan Ada Wang found herself deeply interested in rural education when she was working for her university on educational outreach programs with primary and middle schools in rural Hubei Province. After working in telecommunication engineering industry for two years after college, she decided to continue pursuing rural education in China because she believed in the needs for educational equity in rural China. She joined TFC in 2013 and participated in implementing the CORE project as a TFC fellow. Below, she describes her firsthand experience of the project, addressing these questions: What are fellows' motivations for pursuing community projects? What challenges do fellows face when they implement CORE? What are the roles of TFC fellows, staff and leaders in the development of projects?

Tongji Philip Qian comes from Shanghai, and he pursued a TFC fellowship shortly after he graduated from college in 2013. He intended to join TFC because he enjoyed his previous traveling experience in Yunnan and he was interested in the notion of living in the mountains. More importantly, he trusted that his teaching experience in rural China would help him contemplate his own position as an educator in both rural and urban communities. Phil speaks from the standpoint of a fellow who purposefully resisted pressures to initiate projects and decided instead to continue focusing on classroom teaching. He approaches his writing with these questions in mind: Should fellows be well-rounded? Should they prioritize teaching? To what extent are fellows connected to the local community and aware of local contexts? What is the hierarchy among different types of projects and people within TFC?

Sara Lam is from Hong Kong, and she visited numerous TFC conferences and placement schools in summer 2014 as she was working on her Ph.D. dissertation on education equality in a global context. Because of her research and teaching both in China and in the U.S., she speaks from the perspective of an outside observer with experience of working both as a practitioner in rural schools and as a scholar who has conducted fieldwork in TFC trainings and project schools. She addresses these questions in her writing: What is the purpose of community projects in the context of TFC and TFAll? Are teaching excellence and leadership cultivation complementary or competing goals? Who should lead transformational change to rural communities?

Fan Ada Wang—Projects as a Major Task for Fellows

I taught in an elementary school in Heqing, Dali Bai Autonomous Prefecture in Yunnan Province for the TFC fellowship. Yunnan is located in the mountainous region in Southwest China and it is ethnically diverse: more than twenty-five minority groups including the Bai people live in Yunnan. The Bai people have their own oral dialect and many of them do not speak Mandarin before they go to school. There is significant rural-urban disparity in high school and college attendance, and it is especially severe in remote counties in Yunnan. (Li et al., 2015; Loyalka et al., 2017; Wang et al., 2018). Aiming to eliminate educational inequality in Yunnan, TFC started placing teaching fellows in a number of elementary and middle schools in Dali in 2009. When a group of fellows initiated the CORE project in 2011, it quickly gained strong support from both TFC leaders and local educational bureau, because it could offer an important opportunity for students to use their own local communities to learn. Consequently, fellows in this region have promoted this project on an annual basis. They began the project by mentoring students in their research topic selections, and typical choices in the past years included studying different contemporary professions and learning to imagine feasible and creative business models in the local community (a strong example for the project entailed a thorough investigation on the biological properties of *matsutake* mushrooms which were grown in rural Yunnan but were sent to Shanghai, Beijing, and Tokyo within hours after harvesting). Fellows subsequently formed committees to evaluate and rank student groups. Whereas most participating students would have the chance to present their research findings to parents, school officials, and leaders from the educational bureau, the winning team in each school would be awarded a research trip to a major city which would further enrich their knowledge and broaden their horizons; Some other top-ranked groups (usually the top five) would also receive books or notebooks as rewards.

I participated in CORE in 2014. At the beginning of the second semester during my fellowship, my Program Manager (PM)[1] informed all fellows in our county to put CORE on the calendar soon since it was a traditional event in this region and was promoted as one of the most outstanding projects conducted by TFC fellows. I had heard of it before by its Chinese name, "Letting Our Hometown Become More Beautiful", but I never knew it was a mandatory project. Our PM then proposed that all schools initiate CORE because she believed that local students and teachers would benefit from using another learning method and fellows could build strong skills in leadership, communication, and cooperation by conducting such a complex project.

All three first-year fellows in my school, including me, were reluctant to proceed because this project was not planned by us and it would not be good timing for our school. We had just gone through a hard time at the beginning of our teaching career; the only second-year fellow was absent for the entire first semester due to medical reasons and the fact that we all had to take her course load made our intense schedules even more burdensome. Additionally, the CORE project seemed too time-consuming (preparation usually began in March and the final research trip took place in July or August). We tried to persuade our PM but failed. From her perspective, the point of CORE was to encourage all schools in our county to work together. Because of such pressure from our PM and the second-year fellow (our school could not conduct CORE if she was the only one intending to do so), I finally agreed to initiate the CORE project in our school.

Difficulties came one by one. Firstly, during the fellow meetings, most Chinese teachers in TFC acknowledged that they themselves did not have enough knowledge about how to facilitate research-based projects or project-based learning because most schools in the Chinese educational system did not teach this at all. To solve this problem, we had several training meetings held by an American co-fellow in my elementary school who had experience conducting research and similar projects in college as a student. Secondly, few resources were available to us regarding the previous CORE projects. Consequently, the process designed by some fellows turned out to be too difficult to carry out because people wanted it to be perfect. Fellows also had to fund this project with little support from the financial department of TFC. Unlike small-scale fellow projects, CORE was indeed costly. In the previous years, rewards included a trip to other cities and some fellows insisted that we should not change it to other "less attractive" awards. I actually avoided working on fundraising because I was aware of another tradition which I disliked—a large portion of the money fellows raised came from donations of fellows' families and friends. There was a reason for that. Although the CORE project was well-known within TFC and was marketed on TFC's major media platforms, it was still not influential enough for most foundations or companies to sponsor. TFC also could not support it financially since fellows in many regions were doing various projects at the same time and it was hard to fund them all fairly.

Schools' reactions towards CORE also hindered its development for some fellows. A fellow would be lucky to have school officials who appreciated the value of this project. If not, fellows like us would have to convince local teachers to join the preparation team and to persuade principals to give us time to guide students in their research during school sessions. Due mainly to the fact that I was the person in charge of promoting CORE at my school (my two co-fellows from TFC were American and spoke minimal Chinese[2] and the second-year fellow wanted to focus on judging students' teams), I became automatically responsible for communications with the principal, local teachers, and students.

I then found it challenging to run CORE projects because of my academic load. In the TFC network, situations of teacher shortage varied from school to school. The fellows with less teaching work, like the second-year fellow in my school, were passionate about CORE but fellows like myself and my first-year co-fellows had intense teaching schedules and additional routine jobs assigned by the school. The heavy workload eventually became unrealistic and I began to assume more responsibilities than I should because of the various textures of the situation. I then decided to quit CORE after two months.

The intention of CORE was to create another way of learning beyond the classroom, as I have mentioned at the beginning of this section, but why did fellows like me question the practical value of it? In my opinion, fellows' disappointment in PMs and TFC leaders contributed to this struggle. Fellows did not get enough assistance from TFC and they needed to count on themselves because the support some managers offered was not sufficient. Moreover, PMs prioritized marketing achievement which would show great regional performance and ignored fellows' request of balancing teaching and conducting projects, thus failing to evaluate the feasibility of some works, like CORE, on fellows' behalf. As a result, PMs sometimes simply assigned fellows certain tasks and offered little autonomy of when and how to do it. This unhealthy interaction between fellows and their PMs made obeying the rules and doing the required work a norm in TFC. In my experience, when fellows tried to convince PMs to modify rules in specific cases, usually no changes were implemented because the PMs believed that such rules made TFC a united and organized group. Among all the regulations in TFC, some were questionable yet not negotiable. Is it ironic that TFC believes in the importance of teaching students critical thinking but restrict the critical ideas of fellows?

In conclusion, the CORE projects, along with many other projects initiated by TFC and its fellows, showcase a good intention to develop the skills and abilities of both fellow teachers and students, but they could only produce more impact for everyone if the majority of people involved in the projects worked with enthusiasm, dedication, and most importantly, mutual respect. Otherwise, these projects become just mandatory tasks to furnish a line on the resume of both TFC and the fellows.

Tongji Philip Qian—"Projects" As Undivided Attention to Teaching

For my TFC fellowship, I taught mathematics to eighth graders and art to seventh graders for the first year, and art for the whole school ranging from first grade to eighth grade for the second year. Since my school was located in one of the remote regions of the Dali prefecture, I developed my teaching and mentoring philosophy independently instead of waiting for the bi-monthly visits by my PMs for assistance. Because of my inclination to discuss most of my teaching experience with local educational bureau officers, principals, and co-workers, my perspective regarding TFC might differ from that of other fellows who remained tightly situated in the TFC niche of fellows and staff members. For this writing, I hope to share my thoughts on TFC's desire to encourage fellows to conduct projects which are supposed to embody long-term impacts on the local communities.

In my experience, TFC suggests that fellows should be able to pursue projects which can reach out to not only students but potentially the local community as well. I was introduced to various exemplary projects both in my region and elsewhere. For instance, I understood that the most marketed and talked-about project is CORE in the Heqing region. Students in elementary and middle schools who participated in the CORE project would research the specialties of their home villages (*matsutake* mushrooms, tobacco leaves, silverwares, for example) and share their findings in the forms of oral presentations and writings, and TFC teachers would facilitate their inquiry and collaborate with students to showcase these research findings in a different location such as the state capital Kunming or Beijing (people living in bigger cities are somewhat unfamiliar with the local specialties from remote villages). Since most students never traveled outside the Dali Prefecture, they were enthusiastic about CORE because of a potential field trip. As a result, the process to choose a winning team for the CORE project became extremely selective and at times convoluted.

Since Heqing was one of the first areas which established relationships with TFC,[3] the attitude toward CORE differed greatly by school. Based on my conversations with senior officials from the educational bureau in the prefecture, I learned that some Heqing principals were excited about CORE since they trusted that TFC fellows would be able to excel in *suzhijiaoyu* ("quality education" to improve the humanity of a person) whereas others were more reluctant to execute such projects because they demanded all teachers concentrate on improving test scores. Because of these different priorities, some of my colleagues placed in the Heqing region received limitless support from their schools while other fellows received minimal assistance. Inevitably, the latter group of people faced a dilemma: they were requested by TFC to appreciate and adopt the tradition of carrying out CORE projects even though their placement schools were not responsive. In fact, some fellows in Heqing told me their principal asked explicitly whether the implementation of CORE might lead to any major donations because a number of former fellows located funding to build a new library for the school. Although I do acknowledge and believe that the cynical mentality of this particular principal was an extreme exception, I think that it would not be an exaggeration to state that different principals/schools had contrasting interpretations of the CORE projects.

The pressure from TFC for fellows to prioritize projects was quite consistent for my second year. I received a large number of emails and calls reminding fellows to submit proposals to initiate projects. I was not excited about projects like CORE in my school because I was more interested in designing effective art curricula for my students. As I explained my rationale to my PM, he understood my concern. We eventually agreed that I would opt out of the "program" of projects and would continue to focus on teaching, and I really appreciated the flexibility offered by my PM. In contrast, some fellows did face major problems when they tried to balance both coursework and projects, as our regional fellow meetings usually entailed a note from the PM that maintaining great scores for students was as important as designing fabulous community programs. It implied, in my view, that a small number of fellows might have gotten too excited about their projects and thus overlooked the significance of consistent and superb teaching performance in the classroom. Ultimately, I consider myself to be a teaching fellow instead of a project-conducting social worker.

Throughout my two-year sojourn, I did incorporate many small art workshops into my curricula. Because of my art history background, I took advantage of the era of Minimalism, which had the potential to be universally understood, and invited students to decode seminal artworks such as Sol LeWitt's *Quadrangle* (1974) and Joseph Kosuth's *One and Three Chairs* (1965). Students interacted with my materials with great interest, and most of them found it amusing that LeWitt can transcend mathematics to art and that a photograph, some printed words, as well as an actual chair can all be understood as "chairs" according to Kosuth. And they shared my workshop materials with families and friends. Moreover, I collaborated with an Omaha-based non-profit organization "With Food in Mind" which used art to educate kids from low-income communities about health and food injustice, and I designed a culinary art lecture to third-grader students to encourage them to understand color pigments from local food ingredients. Most importantly, my final week of the fellowship coincided with student graduation, and I invited the graduates to critically consider the different dimensions of future life by listening to David Foster Wallace's commencement speech at Kenyon College in 2015. I would not characterize these short workshops as "projects;" nevertheless, I did see a similarity between conventional programs of community projects and these creative lectures: I trusted that I exposed my students to new methods of seeing and thinking which were not familiar to them. Compared to projects like CORE, my small workshops were more closely integrated into my art curricula; I thus did not have to turn away from teaching.

Three years after my fellowship with TFC, I still find great satisfaction in my teaching experience in rural China, and I have no regret that I never conducted any remarkable projects such as CORE. I am grateful that my students were engaged during my mini-workshops, and their insightful responses to my seemingly unanswerable open-ended questions reciprocally broadened my own horizons. I believe that such small enlightening moments for both me and my students have the potential to eventually snowball to become long-lasting impacts. As TFC is becoming much more geographically diverse and is covering many more regions in China, I start to wonder what their ultimate vision really entails as hundreds of young college graduates are encouraged to move to rural China to teach. Are they really to innovate within the local educational systems? Are they actually to become responsible community leaders? Is it realistic to expect them to be both? Where exactly should the role of TFC be situated in the context of rural communities? These questions become critical for me as an alumnus when TFC abandons its long-established partner schools (including Ada's and mine) and chooses to heavily advertise in major social media platforms about its annual galas and auctions in the Shanghai Shangri-la.

Sara Lam—Placing Projects in the Organizational Context of TFC and Teach For All

During their two years in the classroom, participants of TFAll member organizations are not simply there to be teachers. They have an additional role: to develop skills and gain firsthand experience in low-income schools which will allow them to become more impactful leaders. To what extent do these dual goals—of cultivating teachers and leaders—complement each other?

TFAll's response to this question would be that these two goals are inseparable and interdependent. Teaching *is* leadership. According to Teach For America (TFA), the characteristics of highly effective teaching can be distilled to six "principles one would find embodied by any successful leader in any challenging context" (Farr, 2010, p. 4): (1) set big goals; (2) invest students and their families; (3) plan purposefully; (4) execute effectively; (5) continuously increase effectiveness; and (6) work relentlessly.

According to this perspective, the goal of leadership development fully serves the goal of cultivating outstanding teachers. Developing these leadership skills and dispositions in participants will not only set them up to become impactful leaders as alumni, but are also the same characteristics that participants need to be highly effective in the classroom. While attending the TFC training institute of 2014, I observed that the training TFC provided for new teachers was designed within this *Teaching As Leadership* framework.

The TFAll model is based on the assumption that the experience of teaching in high-needs schools for two years will make participants better leaders. TFA and TFAll founder, Wendy Kopp, envisioned that "corps members who go would go into other fields would remain advocates for social change and education reform ... because of their experience teaching in public schools, they would make decisions that would change the country for the better" (2003, p. 7). Echoing this idea, a member of TFC's core leadership team explained that leaders of education reform should have expertise in education, and that fellows gain this expertise by spending two years as classroom teachers. Although the TFAll model assumes that the dual goals of cultivating leaders and teachers are complementary, in my research fieldwork, I observed some tensions between the dual goals of cultivating teachers *and* leaders in the context of TFC.

One of these tensions is a result of how early TFC fellows are expected to step up as leaders of community impact. TFAll public materials primarily speak about accelerating the leadership impact of alumni. Regarding "collective leadership development" and "community impact", the TFAll website reads: "Informed by their experiences, network alumni go on to become career teachers, school and district leaders, policymakers, advocates, and entrepreneurs who work together with many others to change systems and disrupt the status quo for children in disadvantaged communities" (Teach For All, n.d.). In TFC, the expectation of leading community impact is not only for alumni who have completed the two-year fellowship, but rather comes as early as the first year of teaching. TFC expects fellows to make an impact on communities by initiating and leading projects during their fellowship period. Before fellows enter their placements, they participated in training sessions that prepared them to initiate such projects. The summer training also included testimonials from and stories about fellows who had developed successful projects. The CORE project was repeatedly brought up as an exemplar. Fellows were asked to envision types of community projects they want to launch although they had not yet been to their placement sites. Many first year fellows expressed eagerness or experienced pressure to start a project during their first year, often in addition to expectations that they contribute to existing projects initiated by second year fellows. The first year of teaching is difficult for most teachers. TFC fellows face additional challenges beyond those experienced by most teachers. They have received only several weeks of training before entering their placements. Most of them need to navigate vast differences between their cultural backgrounds and those of the communities where they teach. The expectation that they also play a leadership role in impacting the community compounds these challenges.

A related tension between these dual goals lies in an underestimation of the pedagogic expertise required to become an outstanding teacher. During my fieldwork, I heard staff and leaders of TFC explain that fellows will have overcome their most pressing teaching difficulties within the first year or even first semester of teaching. This idea is used to justify the expectation that they are ready to take on other leadership roles outside of their teaching responsibilities shortly after entering the classroom, such as providing teaching training to other fellows and launching projects. Fellows whom I interviewed, meanwhile, expressed a very different perspective on their professional development needs. Many second year fellows felt that they still had much room for improvement in their teaching. Some felt unprepared to take on the training roles they were asked to and wished instead to receive pedagogic training from more experienced educators. TFC's expectations for fellows to become strong teachers within one semester or year is not only contrary to the realities of fellows' experiences in the classroom, but also contributes to the deprofessionalization of the teaching profession by underestimating and devaluing the expertise required of teachers and education leaders.

A final tension about the dual goals is between empowering outsiders to lead change in rural communities and supporting the agendas of local community leaders. Who should lead change to marginalized communities? Wendy Kopp's impetus for founding TFA is based, in part, on the assumptions that "top college graduates" will be the leaders of tomorrow, *and* they lack the experience in low-income communities that would ground their leadership in a commitment to addressing inequities. From this perspective, there are two ingredients for social change leadership. The first is elite leadership pathways—"top college graduates" have pathways to leadership resulting from the resources and elite social networks that they can access at prestigious universities. The second is understanding of and commitment to tackling social inequity. The TFAll model recruits individuals who already have access to leadership pathways, further strengthens their pathways, and adds the second ingredient of understanding of inequity. An alternate model would be to connect with marginalized communities, which are already rich with people who have deep understandings of inequity and are deeply committed to making change, and make elite leadership pathways accessible to them. A high level TFC leader explained in an interview that TFC would not consider initiating programs to accelerate the leadership of local educators in their project sites because recent college graduates are more suitable.

Yet, in my own experience of working in rural communities and schools, I have had the honor of meeting inspiring rural teachers who *are* taking the lead to change their communities. Zheng Bing, a former rural teacher in Shanxi Province, founded a network of village cooperatives that now encompasses over 40 villages. The cooperatives provide agricultural education, preserve local traditional culture, cultivate women to become community leaders, organize microloans, improve the physical environment of their communities and more. In Shandong Province, Cui Qisheng was appointed as principle of a failing rural middle school. Under his leadership, the school not only became the top ranked school in the area but also developed its own pedagogical model that challenges students to be active and independent leaders. Teachers and education leaders from around the country go to learn from their model. In Guizhou province, one teacher saved the one-room school of a remote mountain village from being closed amidst a wave of rural school consolidation. School closings in that region often resulted in increased drop out due to the dangerous trek students would have to make to get to school each week and the increased expenses of boarding at school during the school week. She committed to teaching there long-term, even though that required her to live apart from her own family in a dilapidated and leaky wood shack. Due to her commitment and advocacy, the local government not only agreed to keep the school open, but also build a safer concrete school building to replace the original school room. I can only imagine the impact that rural leaders like these could have if the vast resources of TFAll were mobilized in support of *them* instead of focusing on elite but temporary outsiders.

The projects initiated by TFC fellows have, no doubt, brought benefits to their students and communities. Yet, the role that projects and leadership development plays in TFC raises both practical and ethical questions. To what extent does the focus on cultivating fellows' leadership detract from their ability to be good teachers for their students? Should top college graduates be the ones who lead change in marginalized rural communities? How can we further empower rural teachers and leaders who are making positive changes in their communities?

Notes

1. Program managers (PMs) are TFC staff who oversee fellows' teaching performances and serve as bridges for communication between schools, fellows and TFC leaders.
2. For many years, Teach For China recruited teaching fellows from the U.S. and these fellows were not required to have Chinese language skills. TFC recently discontinued the practice of recruiting fellows overseas.
3. When the collaboration was first formed, TFC was then the China Education Initiative (CEI).

References

Farr, S. (2010). *Teaching as leadership*. San Francisco, CA: Jossey-Bass.
Kopp, W. (2003). *One day, all children . . .: The unlikely triumph of Teach For America and what I learned along the way*. New York, NY: Public Affairs.
Li, H., Loyalka, P., Rozelle, S., Wu, B., & Xie, J. (2015). Unequal access to college in China: How far have poor, rural students been left behind? *The China Quarterly, 221*, 185–207.
Loyalka, P., Chu, J., Wei, J., Johnson, N., & Reniker, J. (2017). Inequalities in the pathway to college in China: when do students from poor areas fall behind? *The China Quarterly, 229*, 172–194.

Teach For All. (n.d.). What We do. Retrieved September 6, 2018, from https://teachforall.org/what-we-do.

Wang, L., Li, M., Abbey, C., & Rozelle, S. (2018). Human capital and the middle income trap: How many of China's youth are going to high school? *The Developing Economies, 56*(2), 82–103.

6. Teach For All in Latvia: A Case Study and Warning to the World

ELĪNA BOGUSA AND IEVA BĒRZINA
Latvia

Biosketch

Elīna Bogusa and **Ieva Bērzina** are socially active mothers who have engaged in public discussions on general education content reform in Latvia. They have taken part in several meetings of the Education, Culture and Science Committee of the Parliament (Saeima) dealing with the issues related to education content reform, were participants in public working groups initiated by the Ministry of Education and Science, and submitted their own proposals for the new education content reform Education2030 (Skola2030).

Narrative

Introduction

The Baltic States—Estonia, Latvia, and Lithuania—were the first countries to join the global education network Teach For All (TFAll) in 2008. Latvia was the third country, following Great Britain and Estonia. TFAll's organization in Latvia, known as "Iespējamā misija" ("Possible Mission" or "IM"), was founded with support from the Swedbank and lead by the former COE of Swedbank Ingrida Bluma. Not a relatively new initiative, IM's 10th Anniversary Forum was celebrated on March 8, 2019 (Iespējamā Misija, n.d.-c). The Anniversary Forum was co-funded by the "New Way for New Talents in Teaching," or NEWTT (NEWTT, n.d.). IM is also co-financed by the European Union through the Erasmus+ grant and is run by a consortium of 15 partners, including TFAll.

According to the organization's own words, IM's operational program was developed based on McKinsey's research on general education in developed countries, where educational improvement is linked with developing effective instructional leaders in schools by getting the right teachers to become principals, developing instructional leadership skills, and focusing each principal's time on instructional leadership (McKinsey & Company, 2015; Stepiņa, 2015). That is, the primary focus of IM's approach to education reform is not focused on developing quality teachers, rather, the organization and its supporters are interested in moving novice teachers into and out of the classroom as quick as possible as they elevate themselves into leadership and policymaking decision. IM's approach to teacher education reform and the broader global education reform movement mirrors that of Teach For America (TFA) in their focus on leaders rather than teachers. Accordingly, an IM teacher's role is primarily to be a change agent for the promotion of educational and social changes in a classroom, in a school's internal culture, and for a whole society. In many ways, the entrenchment of IM alumni across leadership and policymaking positions in Latvia represent a case study of what happens when TFAll and TFA accomplish their agenda on a national scale.

In fact, about twenty IM alumni are currently senior experts working on an education content reform project, Education2030 (skola2030.lv), that seeks to redesign the curriculum for general education in all levels—preschool, basic, and secondary school in Latvia. The education content reform project is led by the longtime COE (director) and Board member of IM—Zane Oliņa.

Based on IM information, 158 people have been recruited to become change agents in schools and society from 2008 to 2018 and the amount donated to IM during these ten years is €2,808,510. Based on the data from the Ministry of Education and Science, there were 28,520 teachers of general education in Latvia during the 2016–2017 academic year. Compared to the population of general education teachers, IM recruits (over a combined period of 10 years) compile only 0.6% from the total number of teachers yet they constitute a large number of reformers within powerful leadership and decision making positions.

In our view, research on the impact of IM in Latvia is severely lacking. There exist only a few Master's Thesis studies on IM's role in leadership and mentoring in Latvian schools. There is no research on the effectiveness of the IM program linked to pupil learning, learning outcomes, or any comparative studies comparing schools that have, and don't have, IM teachers. To that end, this chapter provides an anecdotal discussion on how IM has shifted the educational landscape in Latvia from our perspective as parents, citizens, and educational activists and raises significant questions and concerns about the actions and agendas of the IM organization and TFAll more broadly.

Education System in Latvia

Since 1991, Latvia's education system has been functioning under continuous reform following the fall of the Soviet Union and the independence of the Republic of Latvia was re-established. Educational policy has been greatly influenced by the recommendations of the World Bank, the Foreign Investors' Council in Latvia (The Foreign Investors' Council in Latvia, n.d.), the Soros Foundation Latvia, OECD (The Organisation for Economic Co-operation and Development), and other global actors. The new national education strategy 2021–2027 (OECD, 2018) will be elaborated in line with OECD's expertise. TFAll, or IM, is currently playing an outsized role in the reform of the general education content and teacher education reform in universities across Latvia.

The Latvian education system consists of pre-school education, basic education, secondary education, and higher education. General education in Latvia lasts 12 years, consisting of a compulsory 9 years of basic education and 3 years of secondary education. Additionally, pre-school education for ages of 5–6 is also compulsory in Latvia. Basic education stages comprise general basic education (grades 1–9) and vocational basic education. Secondary education stages comprise general secondary education, vocational secondary education, and vocational education. Higher education comprises both academic and professional study programs (AIC, n.d.).

The education system is administered at three levels—national, municipal, and institutional. The Parliament (Saeima), the Cabinet of Ministers, and the Ministry of Education and Science are the main decision-making bodies at the national level. The Ministry of Education and Science is the education policy development and implementation institution that oversees the national network of education institutions, sets educational standards, and determines teacher training content and procedures. The tuition fee for pre-school, basic, and secondary education in a state or municipality-funded educational establishment is funded through the national or municipal budget. Comparatively, a private educational institution may set a tuition fee for providing education (Ministry of Education and Science, n.d.).

The National Centre for Education and the State Education Quality Service are the main authorities responsible for the content and the quality of general education (National Centre for Education of the Republic of Latvia, n.d.; State Education Quality Service, n.d.). Inga Juhnevica, the head of the State Education Quality Service, has been a longtime Board member of IM, and is the member of Consultative Council of IM at the time of the writing of this chapter. Zane Olina, the longtime COE and Board member (until 2018) of IM was contracted by the National Education Centre to implement the education content reform project Skola2030.

Foundation of "Iespējamā Misija"

IM is registered as a public benefit organization which is a non-governmental organization (Lursoft, n.d.). It has declared itself as a public benefit organization established by entrepreneurs, or a national-level corporate social responsibility initiative in the field of education in Latvia, which seeks to promote change in public schools by attracting talented young people to work as teachers (special change agents) for two years. IM is also registered as educational institution in the Register of Educational Institutions. The Register is managed by the State Education Quality Service (NIID.LV, 2015).

Latvia's inclusion in the global umbrella of TFAll was enacted by bankers and others working within the Open Society Institution (Soros Foundation). IM was founded in 2008 by Swedbank, the largest private bank in Latvia, "Lattelecom," the largest telecommunications company in the Baltics, and "The Partners in Ideas Foundation" (PIF) ('*Ideju partneru fonds*' in Latvian) (Iespējamā, n.d.-b). In 2006, PIF was created as result of the Baltic-American Partnership Program operated by the Baltic America Partnership Foundation, which was established in 1998 by the United States Agency for International Development (USAID) and the Open Society Institute (OSI). The Baltic-American Partnership Program director and the program director of the Soros Foundation in Latvia Ieva Morica, Local Expert Council Atis Zakatistovs, and the departing COE of Swedbank Ingrida Bluma founded the PIF. As reported by the Baltic America Partnership Foundation, "In 2006, after a study tour to the United States to look at emerging models of 'venture philanthropy,' the BAPP Latvia established this new grant making and technical assistance institution, intended to serve as a central part of the BAPP's legacy for Latvian civil society" (BAPF, 2008, p. 31). The first project implemented by PIF was the creation of IM, "an initiative modeled on Teach for America, to train and place young teachers in the public school system. The project already initially garnered tremendous public attention and support, with close to $1 million dollars in private sector funding secured for its activities" (BAPF, 2008, p. 31). And, as noted above, since its inception in 2008 through 2018, IM has received €2,808,510 in donations.

Similar to other philanthropic efforts (Reckhow, 2013; Reckhow & Snyder, 2014), Swedbank has declared education as the main area of influence of its social responsibility in Latvia. They noted, "We are convinced that Latvia's path towards growth lies specifically in education. It is this area where we develop our initiatives and work in long-term partnerships" (Swedbank, n.d.). Swedbank has since donated €100,000 to IM every year. Not surprisingly, Karlis Kravis, the current director of IM, is also an IM alumni and youth segment manager for Swedbank (LinkedIn, n.d.).

IM Leadership Development Program

As an educational institution, IM implements its own IM Leadership Development Program. Inga Juhnevica, the Head of the State Education Quality Service, has served on the IM Board Member for numerous years, and she is currently a member of IM Consultative Council at the time of this writing.

The official aim of IM is "to attain participation of young, talented and leadership endowed university graduates in field of education, in order to create a positive and progressive environment in schools, raise the prestige of the teachers' profession, increase students' motivation to learn, to become active members and creators of society" (Partners in Ideas Foundation, n.d.). Additionally, "IM is looking for those who want to be inspiring teachers and future leaders—change agents and enactors of changes, who demonstrate enthusiasm and desire to realize positive changes in education; for those who will be able to continue program aims after their two-year commitment in the classroom" (Latvijas Universitate, 2015). IM expects its alumni will impact the quality of education in Latvia not only being teachers, but much more as future school directors, NGO leaders, education entrepreneurs, and public officials. Alumni form the IM Community—the network based on these common values and aims. Many educational initiatives are implemented based on these ties—projects, lobbing in governmental level, educational business companies, etc. in a similar fashion to what has been observed in the United States following the TFA model (Brewer, Hartlep, & Scott, 2018). In this way, the IM Leadership Development Program is implemented in a similar fashion to other TFAll programs around the world (Iespējamā, n.d.-a). The following is the cycle of the Leadership Development Program:

- **Recruitment in 4 rounds**: application letter, phone interview, presentation of a demo lesson, and face to face interview. Applicants have to have at least a bachelor's degree (may be the final year student). Recruitment is based on vision about the personal importance of every student. They are portrayed as superheroes who are able to promote the growth of every child, to make positive changes in every school, and to improve the future of society just now. By working in school every IM participant changes the lives of 70–400 pupils, according IM.
- **Placement in schools**: IM doesn't focus specifically on marginalised social groups and regions like other TFAll or TFA programs. Rather, IM says "it is a movement working to provide the qualitative education for every child in Latvia, to make the necessary changes in classrooms, schools and in society" (Iespējamā, n.d.-b). The school and teaching

subject assignment for an IM teacher is chosen in cooperation with the State Education Quality Service. IM teachers are placed in schools that have confirmed their readiness to change their institution and willingness "to become an effective learning organisation and incubator for all new teachers in Latvia" (Iespējamā, n.d.-d).

- **Summer Academy**: during a six-week period in the summer, the new participants learn the necessary knowledge and skills to start work in schools in September of that year.
- **1st year in school**: on the first of September, participants start to work full time jobs as teachers in the public schools. The central task in the Leadership Development Program is to acquire skills such as how to lead learning, how to lead others, and how to lead himself or herself. During this time, they continue to study in the IM Leadership Development Program every other Friday and Saturday. In the IM Leadership Development Program, at least 650 academic hours are devoted to acquiring teaching and management skills and at least 1,000 academic hours of pedagogical practice. Graduating the program, alumni receive a certificate that allows them to continue to work as teachers if they choose (which, again, is not the primary objective or focus of the organization). This practice is similar to other TFAll and TFA placement regions that require their teachers to engage in formal training during their temporary license status. The IM teachers are supported by curator, mentor and couching during the time of program. They receive additional grant to the salary in amount of 200 euros every month and personal computer or tablet.
- Summer Event: during the summer vacation, a one-week training event is held for IM teachers. At the end of training the stories of success are shared with the new, incoming teachers.
- **2nd year in school**: IM teachers continue to attend IM Leadership Development Program. The main focus is to develop their skills of leadership and management. During the 2nd year of the program, IM teachers have to lead their own change initiative at school level.
- **Graduation**: After a two-year period, there is a graduation. Impact stories about alumni successes and challenges are obligatory before the official graduation. Alumni impact stories are organized as special public events. Graduating from the program, alumni receive a certificate allowing them to continue to work as a teacher. IM Leadership Development Program is equivalent to teacher preparation programs in pedagogical high school and universities in Latvia.
- **IM Community**: alumni are inducted into a network based on common values and reform aims. Many educational initiatives are ultimately

implemented by drawing on these connections—projects, lobbing at the governmental level, educational business companies, etc. IM participants are highly motivated to make changes in the field of education. They are continually reassured that they play a crucial role in reimagining the national educational system.

Impact of IM at National Level

As a result of their concerted efforts to leverage their alumni network, IM has become an outsized voice in national policymaking and is involved in three important governmental working groups on education reform: (1) on education content reform or teaching standards in general education, (2) on measuring teacher quality, (3) and on teacher preparation programs in universities.

For example, IM has been able to gain control and shape much of the conversation and reform associated with the Education Content Reform that was launched in 2016. The project, led by the National Centre for Education (which is the public administration institution directly subordinated to the Minister of Education and Science), and funded by the European Social Fund draws from a funding sources of 18 million Euros. Additional supporters of the reform effort are, once again, Swedbank, the founder of IM, and Edurio which is an IM alumni-founded company for education quality assessment. About twenty alumni who are characterized as "senior experts" are working on the education content reform project Education2030 (Skola2030) that is tasked with establishing the new standards for general education in all levels—preschool, basic, and secondary school (Teach For All, n.d.). The Education Content Reform project is led by the former longtime CEO of IM—Zane Olina. The reform is implemented in line with OECD Education 2030 from one side and the IM approach from other side. As a result, the border between the public educational system and IM movement has almost entirely disappeared. During IM's 10th Anniversary Forum, IM was heralded as real champion of education content reform for Skola2030. The project manager, Zane Olina, said: "The approach of Skola2030 is the same one as IM approach only dressed in other words" (iespējamā Misija, 2019). In an additional sign of blurred boundaries, the official website of TFAll the IM story "Influencing Policy Making at the National Level" from TFAll's "10th Anniversary Report" is linked with the website of Skola2030 (https://www.skola2030.lv/).

Swedbank is not only a donor to the Skola2030 reform but also is an active participant in the redesign of the educational content. In March of 2017, Swedbank signed a cooperation agreement with the National Center for Education on integrating economic education issues into the general and vocational education process. On March 5, 2019, the President of Latvia, Raimonds Vejonis, opened the school program "Ready to Life" in the Riga Castle (Latvijas Valsts Prezidents, 2019). The program was jointly implemented by Swedbank and IM. "Today, in modern changing world, the task of education is not only to provide knowledge, but also to develop skills and shape personality of every person," Vejonis said.

Education content reform is accompanied by parallel reforms focused on teacher preparation in universities. Once again, IM is one of the key partners as they were officially nominated by the Government (the Cabinet of Ministers) to participate in the development of the reform efforts as the organization serves on the ad-hoc Consultative Council for Innovative Teachers' Preparation lead by the Ministry of Education and Science (Cabinet of Ministers, 2018). Because of the decision handed down by the Cabinet of Misters, universities are obligated to involve IM "experts" in working groups tasked with creating new study programs associated with teacher preparation. The reform of teacher training is yet another artifact of IM's vision about change agents working in every school.

IM has also been included in the Monitoring Board of European Social Fund's project "Development of a system of quality monitoring of education" (Ministry of Education and Science, 2018). In 2018 the "European Citizen's Prize," the award for exceptional achievements was awarded to IM (European Parliament, n.d.). Only Members of the European Parliament have the right to submit nominations—one per member each year.

Conclusion

Since the very beginning of IM in Latvia, the goal of the organization has been to influence and determine the direction of the national education system. This has largely been accomplished as IM has become the practical implementer and referee of the project to reform curriculum content. And as the organization has become a co-partner of universities seeking to develop new study programs for teacher preparation, their involvement has become further entrenched at all levels of education across Latvia. The goal of IM to move alumni into leadership positions and spread IM dogma has also been realized and Latvia thus serves as a unique case study of what happens when TFAll and TFA realize their agenda. As New Orleans is a case study of a full charter takeover of a city's public schools, Latvia serves as an international case study on the implications of TFAll accomplishing their goals to standardize education and deregulate teacher preparation. Given IM's firm establishment within the policymaking apparatus, it would appear that the organization is primed to continue such reforms. Marite Seile, the CEO of IM, was appointed Minister of Education and Science in Latvia and went to no effort to hide her ideological orientation noting that she, "promised to retain [IM's] values as minister [stating]: 'My goal is to help to introduce them into Latvia's education system'" (Teach For All, 2014). The ascendancy of Seile to this high position has further reinforced IM's hold on educational policymaking in Latvia for years to come.

References

AIC. (n.d.). System of education. Retrieved March 18, 2019 from http://www.aic.lv/portal/en/izglitiba-latvija/system-of-education

BAPF. (2008). *Ten years of grantmaking to strengthen civil society in Estonia, Latvia and Lithuania.* Retrieved from https://www.opensocietyfoundations.org/sites/default/files/bapf_20081111.pdf

Brewer, T. J., Hartlep, N. D., & Scott, I. (2018). Forbes 30 under 30 in education: Manufacturing "edu-preneur" networks to reinforce privatization/marketization. *Educational Policy Analysis Archives, 26*(76), 1–39.

Cabinet of Ministers. (2018). Tiesību aktu projekti. Retrieved March 18, 2019 from http://tap.mk.gov.lv/mk/tap/?pid=40444622

European Parliament. (n.d.). Prizes. Retrieved March 18, 2019 from http://www.europarl.europa.eu/at-your-service/en/be-heard/prizes

The Foreign Investors' Council in Latvia. (n.d.). About us. Retrieved March 18, 2019 from https://www.ficil.lv

Iespējamā. (2019). Facebook. Retrieved March 18, 2019 from https://www.facebook.com/iespejamamisija/posts/10157056815581564?__tn__=-R

Iespējamā. (n.d.-a). Iespējamā misija. Retrieved March 18, 2019 from http://www.iespejamamisija.lv

Iespējamā. (n.d.-b). Katrs bērns var! Retrieved March 18, 2019 from http://www.iespejamamisija.lv/par-iespejamo-misiju

Iespējamā. (n.d.-c). Pieredzes forums. Retrieved March 18, 2019 from http://www.iespejamamisija.lv/pieredzes-forums

Iespējamā. (n.d.-d). Piesakiet vakanci. Retrieved March 18, 2019 from http://www.iespejamamisija.lv/piesakiet-vakanci

Latvijas Universitate. (2015). Izglītības programma "iespējamā misija". Retrieved March 18, 2019 from https://www.karjera.lu.lv/studentiem/kid-uznemumi/kid2015uznemumi/iespejamamisija/

Latvijas Valsts Prezidents. (2019). The president of Latvia opens the school program "ready to life" in the Riga castle. Retrieved March 18, 2019 from https://www.president.lv/en/news/news/the-president-of-latvia-opens-the-school-program-ready-to-life-in-the-riga-castle-25701

LinkedIn. (n.d.). Karlis Kravis. Retrieved March 18, 2019 from https://www.linkedin.com/in/karlis-kravis-90752755/?originalSubdomain=lv

Lursoft. (n.d.). Iespejama misija, nodibinajums. Retrieved March 18, 2019 from https://company.lursoft.lv/en/iespejama-misija/40008124084

McKinsey & Company. (2015). *How the world's best-performing school systems come out on top*. New York: McKinsey & Company. Retrieved October 1, 2019 from https://www.mckinsey.com/~/media/mckinsey/industries/social%20sector/our%20insights/how%20the%20worlds%20best%20performing%20school%20systems%20come%20out%20on%20top/how_the_world_s_best-performing_school_systems_come_out_on_top.ashx

Ministry of Education and Science. (2018). Izglītības kvalitātes monitoringa sistēmas izveide un īstenošana. Retrieved March 18, 2019 from https://www.izm.gov.lv/lv/fondi/es-strukturfondi/izm-istenojamie-projekti/izglitibas-kvalitates-monitoringa-sistemas-izveide-un-istenosana

Ministry of Education and Science. (n.d.). The education system in Latvia. Retrieved March 18, 2019 from https://izm.gov.lv/en/education/education-system-in-latvia

National Centre for Education of the Republic of Latvia. (n.d.). Home. Retrieved March 18, 2019 from https://visc.gov.lv/en/

NEWTT. (n.d.). Welcome to NEWTT! Retrieved March 18, 2019 from http://www.newtt.eu

NIID.LV. (2015). Iespējamās misijas līderības attīstības programma. Retrieved March 18, 2019 from http://www.niid.lv/niid_search/program/19358

OECD. (2018). OECD skills strategy: Latvia. High level skills strategy seminar. Retrieved March 18, 2019 from https://www.izm.gov.lv/images/starptautiska_sad/High-Level-Skills-Strategy-Seminar-Latvia_final.pdf

Partners in Ideas Foundation. (n.d.). Our projects. Retrieved March 18, 2019 from http://www.idejupartneri.lv/en/our-projects/

Reckhow, S. (2013). *Follow the money: How foundation dollars change public school politics*. Oxford: Oxford University Press.

Reckhow, S., & Snyder, J. (2014). The expanding role of philanthropy in education politics. *Educational Researcher, 43*(186), 186–195.

State Education Quality Service. (n.d.). About us. Retrieved March 18, 2019 from https://ikvd.gov.lv/en/

Stepiņa, K. (2015). Ingrīda blūma: Latvijā skolotāju profesija netiek novērtēta Retrieved March 18, 2019 from https://www.db.lv/zinas/ingrida-bluma-latvija-skolotaju-profesija-netiek-noverteta-441883

Swedbank. (n.d.). Society. Retrieved March 18, 2019 from https://www.swedbank.lv/about/swedbank/about/contributionToSociety?language=ENG#

Teach For All. (2014). Latvian partner CEO to lead ministry of education. Retrieved March 18, 2019 from https://teachforall.org/news/latvian-partner-ceo-lead-ministry-education

Teach For All. (n.d.). About. Retrieved March 18, 2019 from https://teachforall.org/about#27101

7. Meritocracy and Leadership: The Keys to Social and Educational Change According to Enseñá por Argentina

VICTORIA MATOZO AND ADRIANA SAAVEDRA

Argentina

Biosketch

Victoria Matozo is a PhD student in Social Sciences at the University of Buenos Aires (UBA), a professor of the University of Buenos Aires and Universidad del Salvador (Argentina), and a researcher of the Instituto de Investigaciones Gino Germani, holding a doctoral Scholarship of the National Council of Scientific and Technical Research (CONICET, Argentina). Her research interests are digital technologies and appropriation of young people, discourse analysis, education policies and other topics related to youth, inequality and education.

Adriana Saavedra holds a Bachelor degree in Social Communication Sciences (University of Quilmes) and a Social Communication Teaching in Media and Higher Education degree (University of Quilmes). She has been teaching in at the secondary level for the past eight years. She is currently completing a Masters degree at the School of Humanities in Education, Languages, and Media at the Universidad Nacional de San Martín.

Narrative

Introduction

This chapter reveals our history, two former Pexas (Professionals of Enseñá por Argentina) in the period 2011–2013, and connects our personal experiences with our appreciation of Teach For All's Argentina project: Enseñá por Argentina (ExA). Although we, Adriana and Victoria, have similar backgrounds, we had different experiences in ExA, whic is why our comments about this NGO (Non-Governmental Organization) will be different. Nevertheless, we have a similar discursive critique about what was "taught" during the program from different points of view about the logic of ExA. Victoria finished the program and returned three years later as a tutor for the SIF (Summer Initial Seminar of Formation 2015), whereas Adriana submitted her resignation after six months of work through ExA in 2012.

This chapter contextualizes the organization "Teach For All" (TFAll) in Argentina and focuses in the inconsistencies between ExA's change theory and innovative pedagogy, and the real teaching training and classroom practices that took place during the second cohort of ExA.

Teach For All in Argentina: ExA

ExA was created in 2008 by Oscar Ghillione, who served as its CEO for eight years. The objective of the TFAll program is to provide every Argentinean child a "quality education," aiming to reduce social and educational inequalities through educational leadership. The organization recruits and trains young professionals designated to work and teach in vulnerable communities. During our Pexa experience, the communities where ExA had a presence were in the city of Buenos Aires and some local municipalities in the province of Buenos Aires called "conurbano bonaerense." To materialize this vision and its mission, ExA staff needs its members to share the organization values as a central part of the TFAll and ExA goal, for example, values such as passion for change, commitment with social reality, sense of responsibility, etc. ExA engages social committed young professionals who feel challenged by the global change objective and proposes them to teach in low income communities as part of a global movement.

Argentinean Education System

In order to understand how ExA enters into the Argentinean education system it is important to briefly explain how this system works. Education in Argentina is considered by law as a public good guaranteed by the State. Every school in Argentina is public but there are two types of management approaches: (1) public management, which is totally financed by the State, free of charge, and secular in its approach to curriculum; and (2) private management that is partially subsidized by the State, charges tuition, and is mainly religious. The subsidy to private schools is diverse (it can be up to 100%). These institutions can be managed in different ways, with their owners, a committee, or a church overseeing the school. While we were Pexas in ExA, the organization was operating in Ciudad Autónoma de Buenos Aires (C.A.B.A.) and the province of Buenos Aires, home to the largest population of teachers in the country.

In our country, teachers are legally protected by the "Estatuto Docente" (teaching statute) and they belong to a tertiary education field: most of them did not attend to university and they were trained and credentialed in Institutos Superiores de Formación Docente (I.S.F.D), specialized centers of teaching.

Both systems are similar but in C.A.B.A. the working hour is a 40-minute class while in the province of Buenos Aires it is a 60-minute class. The salary does not change because of this difference (it is the same salary "per working hour").

It is also important to clarify that teaching positions in public schools are obtained by teachers through "acto público" (a public contest) listed by order of Merit: the teacher with the highest punctuation in the acto público gets the position. Teachers who want to have "hours" of teaching must be enrolled in the system. The main difference between these two geographical areas is that in C.A.B.A. there is the possibility to apply directly to the school if the position is not covered during the acto público and that is how Victoria started teaching in public schools. These cases of "emergency" assignment are covered by Article 66 of the Estatuto Docente.

In private schools, however, hiring is overseen by different members of the institution depending on the type of organization. For instance, teaching positions can be published online in job web pages or other media. The Principal, the Legal Representative, or even the owners of the school could interview and then hire teachers. There are also institutions with a human resources department in charge of this process. Hiring practices are heterogeneous in private schools.

Teaching positions in high school are not in only one school: you take a teaching job "per hour" (teaching hour). For example, Comercial 34 is looking for an English teacher for the 5th course, and the schedule is Mondays from 13:10 to 14:30 and Wednesdays from 17:40 to 18:20. In order to have a decent salary, teachers must teach several courses, often in different schools. That is why it is said that in Argentina most teachers are "taxi teachers" in that they cannot be connected to only one school because they have several institutes they work in (maybe five or six) per week. This is a big problem. Among other concerns, it prevents teachers from getting involved in the institutional life of schools. The number of hours a teacher can have with the full salary is 20 as head teacher in Buenos Aires province, and 40 in C.A.B.A. in any modality. Teaching hours that exceed this amount are paid less by the State as a way to include younger teachers in the system in Buenos Aires province (they can securitize head positions if they have less competition of older teachers with higher scores) and to discourage over-employment in C.A.B.A. But in Argentina, 20 hours is not enough to piece together a respectable salary so teachers are forced to work more for less salary, travelling from one school to the next one. This brief explanation simplifies the Argentinean education system but allow us to introduce the readers to the Argentina reality in order to understand the scope and limitations of ExA within schools in different jurisdictions.

The Beginning of the Road
The first meetings of each cohort were at the Universidad Austral where every activity was "Pexa centered": we had to connect with each other, motivate ourselves, know the organization thoroughly, and understand how special we were to have been selected as Pexas, members of the TFAll global movement. There was a member of Teach For America (TFA) who told us the scope of the organization as a worldwide NGO and the life changing journey (for us and the students) we were about to begin. What the speech was lacking was the theoretical foundations for how we were going to achieve these life changing objectives. Nevertheless, the words were seductive. To have the presence of someone from a global movement, who had travelled to our country (a peripheral country) to start our training process at ExA, made us feel important. It may seem naïve, but those actions made us feel we were involved in a very serious and important movement that would allow us to make a difference for our students.

During this first encounter with ExA, Victoria was not able to participate because she was already working as a teacher in public schools, so she only answered emails and sent requested documentation—she did not participate in several activities that were meant to create a bond among Pexas in an effort to create camaraderie between the members of the group. On the other hand, Adriana participated in and remembers those first encounters as being full of excitement.

The only thing that caught our attention in this process was the fact that the person in charge of assigning teaching positions told us about ExA's decision of selecting many Communication Sciences Bachelors (our degree major) because of the high demand of language practice teachers they had last year. As we were always told that we were selected out of a pool of 2,000 candidates to take part in ExA because of our skills and qualities, we raised a question: were we chosen because of our capabilities or because of a high teaching demand? In any case, we continued the experience motivated by the enthusiasm.

Soon after these first encounters the Seminario Inicial de Formación SIF (Summer Initial Seminar of Formation) began. This summer seminar was named by a Pexa, who was a member of the first ExA cohort, as the "meat mincer", an expression that shocked us: because it was described as a mixed up of concepts and methods focused on products (filling trackers, writing class planning and using motivational techniques) rather than a learning process to became educators.

Summer Initial Seminar of Formation (SIF)

During January of 2012, the SIF consisted of a mixture of training sessions and (non-paid) teaching hours. Every day at 8am we took a private bus that drove us to the SIF: a Catholic private school located in a low-income community, a "villa miseria": low-income neighborhood of shacks, similar to a Brazilian favela. Pexas shared sessions, group assignments, game challenges, breakfast, lunch, and even during the "breaks" we had between-activities. We were motivated to create a song with the rhythm of the "summer hit" which represented our group, goals, and activities. It was an intense schedule.

On the first day, ExA staff welcomed us with our photo and name in a poster. We started the day singing and then raising the Argentina national flag. Motivation was the primary focus and as we engaged in ExA's ideas during the activities we received more positive feedback including notes of affection, letters or encouragement from other Pexas and from ExA staff.

Sessions centered primarily on the ExA mission: to transform the lives of our students through leadership, be a positive leader in the classroom in order to save the system from demotivated teachers (non-ExA teachers), who, lacking "buena onda" (a good mood), did not provide students a quality education. By comparison, our motivation would be what would save students from their current teachers.

During SIF we had to teach classes to kids who needed to remediate different subjects in February.[1] It did not matter if we ourselves did not have the necessary knowledge of the subjects we were supposed to teach, which is extremely troublesome considering that we—without content and subject knowledge—were tasked with teaching the material to students who were already struggling with that subject.

Soon after the SIF began we realized some issues: None of the sessions we took part of were conducted by a national professional educator with experience in low income neighborhoods, vulnerable schools, or even this global network (TFAll). We had several lectures conducted by leaders of non-educative fields, most of them from businesses who had a "client" approach. In fact, a lecturer compared students with clients, and when some Pexas suggested that those words were not synonyms, he respond that wasn't important in the session and political issues were not the center of the lecture. This became an evident breakpoint within our Pexa group. Ideological differences were exposed and politics became an issue that we were supposed to leave outside the classroom.

Other sessions were conducted by first year Pexas to share their experience or a school Principal who was delighted with this new kind of motivational teacher. The most notable was a Principal from a private Catholic school located in the north of Buenos Aires province, which is part of a business group that owns other higher middle-class institutions. This school was one of the most expensive institutions in the area. His stories were all about his suit. He wore a worn out suit every day, to provide a sense of formality for parents, but to show that a suit did not keep him from playing soccer with students. He wanted to make a point: unprivileged kids deserved a principal who wore a suit. It was hard for us to understand this perspective. He was a very motivated person, but his school reality was particular, he had more resources to manage an education institution than other schools in the area. That Principal now works in the national Education Ministry with the former CEO of ExA and some other ExA alumni.

Other concerns centered on the fact that we were not being prepared to teach with a pedagogic training. We were told that as leaders all we needed was a "good and positive" attitude and "believing" that change was possible. In effect, smiling and leadership was enough to change our students' lives. This approach towards education emerged during the SIF when we were forced to teach subjects we were not prepared or trained to teach. Pedagogy, and specificity of the field, was not that important. ExA suggested that we simply had to be motivators, have a strident personality, and create fun activities.

For example, Adriana and other two Pexas had to teach Spanish, specifically syntactic analysis. Pexas haven't studied that topic since they were themselves 11 years old yet they had 48 hours to prepare the lesson. Finally, the group managed to plan a lesson and a Pexa colleague had the idea of including "emojis" in the lesson. If a student gave a right answer, teachers gave him or her a happy emoji. During the observation and evaluation of the class, the tutor was pleased, giving positive reviews not because the content of the class but simply because activity with emojis was fun. It did not matter what you taught (or if you knew the subject and content), just how you did it.

ExA trainers involved in our teaching training process had not worked in vulnerable contexts, even they thought they knew about poor children lives and they presented themselves as education professionals provided with a deep social sensibility. But when we asked about their past and present working career, we noticed that none of them had working experience in the most vulnerable social sectors, they only shared some volunteer experiences "from outside", and not as a working environment or a professional activity. The staff that worked in schools was teaching middle and upper-middle-class students. They taught us what to do, how to act and motivate people based in their own perceptions, not in qualitative research, real practice, or their own working experience.

People involved in the organization did not have political positions or ideas about any topic, including education issues. For us, education is a political act, which includes a lot of ideological commitments such as going to a march or joining a teachers' union strike. Strikes were seen by ExA as lack of commitment to teaching and students, and a non-valid way of protesting. What caught Victoria's attention was that during the initial interviews, staff asked her about her position on this, and she explained she was an active participant in these kinds of political movements. Despite ExA being notably displeased with this answer, she continued with the application process, ultimately becoming a Pexa.

During the SIF, politics were never discussed—or even structural problems of education. But as in every group, there were subgroups where these topics were usually discussed during breaks. Pexas in these subgroups were concerned about politics and education debates that were part of our teaching practice, agreeing there was no place for these issues in the sessions. These subgroups became a place for solidarity among those of us who were questioning the methodology and objectives of ExA.

Despite these subgroups, the aim of the SIF had a cohesion mission: by the end of the summer participants should feel identify with ExA core values, part of the main group. As Pexas spent more than 12 hours together every day we became deeply involved in ExA. Once, we were returning from the SIF to our homes in an ExA school bus which broke down and stopped in the middle of one of the busiest streets in Buenos Aires, Avenida Santa Fé. At the direction of ExA staff and tutors, every Pexa went down the bus and started pushing in an effort to move the bus. Cheering and singing "Yes we can", we managed to move it. In that moment we did not realize it, we were being required to engage in a dangerous activity. Our cohesion as a group blinded us.

SIF finished in February, and we still had a month before classes started to plan instruction and study. We had to accomplish these activities by ourselves, with no mentoring or support. When the school year started some Pexas had a position in only one school, with an acceptable salary and full teaching schedule, while other like us had not the minimum teaching hours promised by the organization. It was evident how influential ExA was in some private schools that did not care about your studies or qualifications: you have to accept the job and "make it work." We also noticed that Pexas who were more aligned to the program and its values had better jobs assigned and a full schedule of teaching hours. Others, like us, were waiting for some positions. We did not have a full schedule and did not earn enough money to maintain ourselves.

The gaps started to emerge, highlighting some additional issues. The organization proposed teaching as an apostleship. The teacher is not a worker entitled to a professional salary, should not be involved in a union, and should not engage in questions about the origin of the inequality he or she aims to eradicate.

ExA reinforces the idea of "social leaders" who are going to change their students' lives and be role models for them. As "transformational" teachers we were going to improve the education system and also other teachers who had lost their passion and motivation,

However this idea never became real: the permanence of educators in the educational system implied only a two-year commitment, therefore it is almost impossible to do an "educative revolution" in a very limited time with teachers that lacked pedagogic training. These ideas pretend to dissolve teaching careers, working with Pexas that only solve superficial problems, do not have a deep knowledge of their working context or are simply incapable to think education and its problems in a political perspective.

It is interesting that in order to do this, Pexas were not trained in pedagogy or more formal training and most of them do not have teaching experience or studies. The mandatory "Profesorado" (formal teaching studies) started after the SIF, when Pexas were already teaching in schools—too little, too late.

ExA pretended us to lead important changes in the schools we were assigned, ignoring the dynamic of Argentinean schools. As previously discussed, in Argentina most teachers are "taxi teachers." Most teachers do not have planning hours or any extra paid time that are not exclusively for teaching hours in the classrooms. The only manner to achieve this objective was to work after hours for free. The approach of teaching resembles volunteer work more than a professional experience. And teaching seemed to be an "accessory" on our leadership career. For those of us who wanted to make teaching our career this seemed contradictory. This description is materialized through our experiences in the organization that are narrated below.

Adriana

In 2011 I had just lost my job. Two years before that, I had finished my degree in social communication and had started the professor's degree at the same university. My studies were almost over so I decided it was my chance to take my first steps in education.

Since private schools hire their staff mostly through recommendations of other teachers, a friend of mine who was working with kids as a volunteer in a "villa miseria" in Solano recommended me for a position as a communication teacher in a school in Quilmes (Buenos Aires province). I was very lucky that year and I was hired. It was only for a few hours and not a lot of money, but it was a way to get experience. In August that same year, I found a flyer at university that invited people to take part in a NGO that worked in the education field. The leaflet was attractive; it made it appear as an interesting project and I decided to apply.

It was a long and wearisome process. The online application asked for a lot of information plus many questions that required detailed answers. That was the first selection test I had to overcome. After that, I had to wait for the results of the exam and, if I passed, I would receive a call. I do not remember how much time went by from the day I first applied to the moment I had the interview, but it was quite a long time—probably over a month. The interview was at a school in Buenos Aires and it was for a group interview. It was a requirement for all applicants to bring a short lesson prepared for the high school level, of about twenty minutes. I remember I had decided to explain the concept of "culture."

When the day finally arrived, I went into the school where there were a few tutors and nine other people like me who expected to take part on that project that sold itself as transformational. The encounter took at least four hours, including a coffee break designed for applicants to get to know each other. Besides giving a lesson, we had to complete question papers, answer questions about our work priorities or what actions we would take in a certain case. After I left, I had a weird feeling. On the one hand, it was the most unusual interview I had ever had and, on the other hand, I wondered what kind of organization would make so many inquiries.

A few weeks later I was informed I had been selected for the next interview. At that point I had to go to the house of one of the members of ExA. The interview was an individual one this time and very personal. The person asked about my motivations for taking part in ExA as well as my motivations towards education, children, and working. Now that I think about it, after all this time, it was only logical that they were looking for people who shared their views on education: people with a career that would set aside everything for a couple of years to later eject themselves from the education system and start working at a private enterprise, may become one of ExA's future sponsors. ExA is simple for those who do not plan to make a long-term living in education. It all seems much easier if I imagine this challenge as only a two year commitment. However, that was not my case, I had the goal of working as a teacher as a permanent job and they knew it.

A few weeks later I received the news that I had been selected for ExA. Out of the 2,000 applicants for the 2012 cohort, only 20 had been selected. Finally, it would be us in charge of transforming education in Argentina. At that moment I felt very happy and relieved. I was happy that for the first time I was going to work at something I really enjoyed, that I had been looking for in my life. I felt relief because during the selection period I had been living alone and surviving out of my savings.

We had a few encounters before the Summer Seminar that would take place at Austral University in Buenos Aires city. There, I would meet the other lucky Pexas. I was a bit anxious and did not know what to expect. It took us a short time to get to know each other and after only two meetings we already knew how each of us felt about certain things, what social class each came from, what were our thoughts concerning education and what universities we had attended. We met a corps member from TFA, who told us about the challenges we would have to face and how it all was worth trying. He said now we were part of a global education network and, of course, that would provide us many personal benefits. I can't recall all the things we did at those encounters. We met participants of the first cohort, prepared a lesson and explored it in front of our new mates, and visited a school inside one of the biggest villas in the city. During the period of time before starting teaching, I stayed in touch with other Pexas, we lived near each other and we used to meet to talk and stay in touch.

In January, one of the most difficult and non-remunerated processes inside of the organisation took place: SIF. The seminar reminded me of the show Gran Hermano (Big Brother). We were bursting with emotions. We spent a huge amount of time together. We got really close. We engaged in teamwork, we had fun together, and took part in the talks ExA offered. Because we spent so much time together, it was impossible, at that point, not to notice more and more the ideological differences between us and ExA. So, I began to ask myself: does ExA have a certain ideology? Or: why did they choose me? The subgroups were noticeable, and not just for us Pexas.

Only one trainer had teaching experience, an English teacher who was from England and an alumni of Teach For Austria, who tried to understand the particularity of Argentinean education but did not have experience in local schools. During that period of time, I had some inconveniences besides some emotional ups and downs: I need to work because I need money to sustain myself but I was not convinced about ExA's concept of education. I was able to connect easily with some of the participants but had intellectual differences with others. For starters, many of them did not seem to perceive any conflicts in the education system nor did they think about the educational processes from an academic point of view. They were incapable of criticizing the organization, none of the events that took place in it were an object of study, observation or criticism for them. Everything was always perfect and wonderful. That created an unbridgeable rift with me. Social injustice has always affected me deeply and during my formal education years I was able to intellectually understand it. To take part in education was, to me, a form of fighting back, a way of transforming the reality of many, of the less advantaged. It was never a calling related to my gender, nor an apostolate I had to fulfill with sacrifice and leadership. To me, teaching was a political act, the means by which to achieve social justice, long postponed in my country. That is where my sensitivity was far away from what ExA needed or expected of me. I was very distanced from many of my fellow participants that were now super fans of TFAll.

I remember wanting to quit many times but I needed an entrance door to education and I thought that was what I was getting, because I kept having very few hours and it wasn't enough to support myself. My biggest crisis was when, in the last two weeks of the process, we had to teach high school students. We were required to help kids study for exams without even knowing the subjects properly ourselves. At that point, I felt unbearable pressure. The group of Pexas I had been assigned to consisted of one that I barely knew and another one whose thoughts about education were the exact opposite of mine. To me, she represented the stereotype of empty leadership ExA expected to create among Pexas. I felt as if I had to lie and say I knew the subjects I was teaching. I was so overwhelmed by the situation that one afternoon I broke down and started crying. And then I made the terrible mistake of telling a trainer how I felt. She did not help me and also forced me to decide: I had to adapt myself to ExA values and ideas or I had to resign. After having little accompaniment and a lot of pressure, I managed to calm down and surrounded myself by those co-participants with whom I felt closer intellectually and emotionally.

The Monday after that episode, given my need of a job, I spoke with my trainer again. I had decided to pretend it had all just been momentary doubts. Now I felt everything I had to explain in my lessons would be magically solved and I was more committed to ExA than ever before. Commitment was their favorite word, so I just had to repeat it. I was able to convince her but not before she humiliated me in every way she could think of: she tried to make me doubt myself, my responsibility and my work.

SIF was over and it was like going through a detox process in which I had come to realize nothing I had learned both in my bachelor or professor's degree had the slightest resemblance with ExA's discourse. As time went by, I started to think I should not worry as much since, once I had my twenty hours in a school, for that was the organization promise, I would follow my own path in the classroom and, of course, would not teach the empty values imparted by ExA. When I dreamt of that outcome I could not imagine that the seminar had not only been a training process (ExA's style) but also a period of evaluation. SIF was a test to prove to ExA who were their most loyal soldiers for their cause. For that reason, those Pexas would benefit by receiving the first hours that became available at a school.

The school year started in March and besides the job I already had from the previous year, I had no news about my placement with ExA. It was only a week after classes had started when I got the call: there was a school for me. It was located at the edge of the largest villa in Buenos Aires. When I went to an interview the person in charge of assigning and getting the class hours from ExA accompanied me. At that time, she asked me to meet at a halfway point and she picked me up with her car. The interview was more of a formality, informative, rather than evaluative. The school already had a few Pexas working there and they were in charge of showing they were there to change education as it was. So much so that they spent more time proclaiming their ideas or projects outside the classroom than their teaching. The lack of teachers that wanted to work at that institution due to the problems it had and the conflictive students made the school very open to receiving these professionals that had no enabling title, no experience but put on airs of greatness.

As we left the school, with days and times already arranged, she told me something I could never forget. She looked at me and pointed: "don't bring that red suitcase, it's too flashy. In addition, you can wear a teacher's apron, so they can identify you." She took for granted that the color red would attract poor people as it does to bulls, to animals. To wear a noteworthy item was equivalent to getting mugged. She stigmatized the community in an unbelievable way, more even if we think how these people claimed to be the defenders of the vulnerable. I just said "okay", I knew I could not argue with her, I could not try to explain. Today it is seven years now that I have been working in that community. I went back with my red suitcase and never had to regret a single incident. Yes, it is a difficult place to work at, the student body is complicated and not anyone can teach there due to the complexity of the situations you have to face as a teacher. It is all about committing yourself, body and mind, being patient, dealing with the lack of materials, and many other things. But I am convinced I would never be working in education if I didn't strongly believe that the context we are born in do not determine who we are as human beings. It is not about leadership or laughs and mambo jumbo songs, it is about hard work, effort, time and, above all, education—education of and for the children and education of and for the teachers.

Taking the hours offered by ExA was not free. They need to know they are transforming education. They ask you not only to work as a teacher but also to fill out and complete their "trackers", which allow them to subjectively evaluate your progress and the progress of your students. It is terribly bureaucratic work that makes no sense. You are the target of unproductive remarks that only tell you your students are being poorly educated, how badly they behave, and how lucky they are to have you as a teacher. The point is never to give you teaching tools that might help you in taking your first steps inside the classroom. Anyone who works in teaching knows how much we learn from empirical experience and how we are nourished from other teachers' knowledge. Teachers who, contrary to what we had learned from the organization, are not the government's parasites.

For my first inspection I fulfilled ExA's goals. I filled out the tracker and sent my daily classroom lesson plans. It was around April or May and I had only gotten four out of the twenty hours promised. I was starting to worry about my financial future and the fact that I couldn't hold on to this part-time job for much longer since there was no real support from ExA. At the end of the lesson, my trainer approached me and we spoke about the great difficulties of classrooms at that school, how many kids there were and how noisy it was. When we took the bus together, nothing stopped her from making all kinds of negative remarks and using the most colorful adjectives to talk about the community. Not a single thing she said was educationally useful, it only confirmed once again what I already knew about the organization and its members: from the CEO to the trainers, they knew almost nothing about education or the vulnerable communities in which they sent ExA Pexas. Nothing about the difficulties they had to sort, their expectations, their pain or their joy. All in all, ExA knew nothing about these people's lives. I confirmed that the social injustice they claimed to want to eradicate through joy was not something that concerned them politically. They did not care about the causes of that injustice; their job was to make us realize we were not in the position of questioning about it nor to look for the root of the problem and help eradicate it. It was not our job to empower our students but to make them submissive towards those who are enabled and leaders—in this case, us.

After some time, I had no news from ExA. I sent an e-mail to the CEO expressing my dissatisfaction with the hour assignment, the organization requirements, and I literally told him I had nothing to eat because I needed to work. The answer was no different than everything in ExA—understanding but it solved nothing. I applied for a "transitional funding", as the organization calls it, but, of course, I did not get it. By that point, I was terribly upset with the way they proceeded and their precepts. It was obvious to me I did not belong there and they sure made me feel it.

Soon thereafter I decided to talk with my principal. I told her I had arrived there through ExA but no longer felt represented by the organization, neither did I share its ideas or values. I asked what would become of my work situation if I decided to leave the organization and she answered I could continue working there for as long as I desired. Relieved, a few days later I turned in my resignation to ExA. I was not the first one to quit the program, there was another before me but we never knew what happened to that person. For that reason, I decided to make my resignation public and I attached the letter they make you write with the reasons for which you terminate the contract. That way, nobody would be able to speak for me or speculate about my reasons for leaving.

After that, I had to go to the office to hand over a copy of my resignation letter. I was received by my ExA trainer. In this last meeting she claimed not to understand any of my reasons to leave and tried to blame me for it, but she quickly realized I had strong convictions and nothing she could say would change my mind. A few minutes later, I left the room where I had to give my reasons and closed that door forever.

Victoria

I have been teaching informally since I was 17 years old and formally since 2007. My mother and other members of my family are teachers, so education has been a central topic of interest and debate all my life. In 2011 after several years having two jobs, always a teacher's job and a more "communication professional" job, I decided to dedicate my career to teaching. That was how I discovered ExA online.

It was a time that I was trying a lot of things and sending out a lot of job applications, so the ExA process did not seem intense to me at the beginning. The staff seemed very comprehensive, as they allowed me to skip some sessions and encounters because I was already teaching. The SIF was intense, but I was open to learning new educational approaches and perspectives. As a chance to increase working hours ExA seemed the right place for me to be.

During my two years in the organization I had a different experience than Adriana but some beliefs are similar. Here I am not only telling my story, I am also trying to analyze this program from four central topics and how these were issued by the organization.

The first topic that caught my attention was the conception of "teaching" the organization had while I was a Pexa. It resembled to me to be understood as a volunteer experience as we were to "put the children first", that meant not to participate in teachers' strikes, working for free if it was necessary, and not participating in teachers' unions or political issues. But the reality was that I was already involved in these activities as I had been a teacher for years before entering ExA with a personal working experience more related to teaching as a political activity. I have always recognized these actions as part of the teaching profession but as I said before, the conception of a teacher's role was different in ExA—the teacher is to be more docile and controllable.

The professionalization of teachers (professors as specialists) was replaceable with a "good attitude." This caused lots of problems in the organization and I think it was the first deficiency of the teacher training. The focus on leadership displaced the teaching practice issue. I recognize that my experience as a Pexa was very different from my experience as a mentor. In 2016 I worked as a Tutor in the SIF, and ExA invited speakers more professionalized in teaching, as many of them worked in Universidad de San Andrés and public educative offices. I think there was an improvement in the quality of teacher training but it still lacked a more professionalized perspective.

This brings me to the second topic. The role of public policies and the context in ExA. I understand that when (and where) the States are not present, NGOs cover the empty space by providing the goods or services for vulnerable populations and the institutions that are not addressed by the governments. But the logic of NGOs sometimes is too far from the public institutions' logic, and that is what I noticed in ExA.

The nonpolitical (or apolitical) stand of ExA lead to a vision about the lower classes that was not structural, so the explanation for how there are students with less opportunities was meritocratic. "If they try hard enough, they will succeed" was the message we were told by the organization and encouraged to reinforce to students. I think is important to analyze this conception from a human rights perspective. Public services, such as public schools, are a State domain that sometimes is surrogate to private organizations. But as the institutions can be under private management, education in Argentina is a public service. This attaches the service of education with the right of being educated. The State must provide education to every person from 4 to 18 years old. If we consider education as a right, the job of teachers is to guarantee this right. When we do not take into consideration this right, as some NGOs logic does, the meritocratic logic ignores the right of being educated and kids who lack social and economic opportunities (structural problems) are burdened to, themselves, overcome this reality and just try harder to get out of poverty.

This meritocratic logic is not always outspoken, it often works through the practices and is unnoticed by the actors. I do not think this issue is problematized, labored, or discussed in ExA because it works under an invisible mechanism. My biggest problem in the organization was exactly that: to say what was not said, more exactly to propose a discussion of a topic that was not assumed as an issue for the actors. During 2013, many of the schools I worked for were "taken" by the students: institution staff and teachers were forbidden to enter the building and activities were stopped at schools. I presented this issue to my ExA mentors and the solutions they gave me was to teach my classes in another space (a club, a park, etc.). I did not agree with this proposal because it is not legal to congregate students outside school and give classes that are part of the curriculum outside the institutions, especially as students were minors and the insurance did not cover (me and even students) during these activities. As Pexas and mentors insisted that State dispositions and rules were not important, I was disappointed to realize the logic I explained before: we had to keep working, no matter what, with the idea that politics do not matter and if we try hard the students will get good results. The intention is not to "blame" the actors, only to expose the logic that is hidden in the acts of this NGO, that sometimes include the recruitment of actors.

This leads me to a second story that shows this meritocratic idea and introduces my third topic of discussion: the conception of the "other." I had problems in a low-income neighborhood school: there were students who stole from me, kids with heavy drug problems, and very particular and vulnerable family and social situations. When a ExA tutor came to my class to observe, she noticed how hard it was to handle these students, but she focused in two areas. First, she told me that the material was not clear. I had made photocopies of some activities handwritten by me, and she told me that I had to bring the best quality materials for the students typed on a computer. I agree with that, but I was working in four schools at the time, from 7:45 am to 9 pm, travelling from one neighborhood to the other and I did not have time to prepare it. My tutor did not recognize this taxi teacher effort and asked me to work harder, again comparing teaching profession to an apostleship, not a job, and unseeing a structural problem of the education system and exposing the ExA logic of if you try, you can. But her second recommendation was more shocking. As we talked about the students' drugs and drinking problems the solution was to "ask the students to get closer to God." Education in Argentina is secular (I reminded her of that), and that school had a high percentage of immigrants that could have or not the same religion of this trainer. There was a thoughtlessness of the other, his/her personal situation and also her/his beliefs. Her perspective seemed to be a "superiority" point of view that considered the student as someone who lacks education and "proper" ideas and had to be guided towards "the right" way. I am not saying that all Pexas and staff members had a "White savior complex," in fact this tutor worked less than a year in ExA and the organization was not very happy with her job. But what I try to point out is that the logic behind ExA opens the entrance in education to professionals that not always share the same approach to education of the organization.

Finally, I want to address here the composition of Pexas and ExA staff. During my Pexa experience our conceptions felt out of place but in the time I worked as a tutor most staff and Pexas had a structural view of the educative problem in Argentina and were not meritocratic orientated. These two styles of members that we could call "volunteer teachers" and "political teachers," were always present in the organization. The difference is not always the educational background, it is the conception of teaching, schools, and students members have. On the other hand, if they believe their job was a more professionalized activity, appreciate the realities of students from a structural perspective and thought about teaching as a political tool of change, they could be considered political teachers. These types did not appear in a pure state but define two perspectives that were confronting in all ExA activity. Of course, this is a personal, simplified and very *ad hoc* classification to make a point about different perspectives and dissidences inside ExA. As I took part as a staff member it wouldn't be fair to say that my voice was not heard, it was not the main perspective they took but I have to recognize that if you are willing to take part in ExA the organization tries to integrate different points of view, even if they not succeed. I also recognize that Adriana's voice was not heard during our Pexa experience, and that really hurt me as Adriana was a valuable asset to the organization, a great teacher with a global perspective about education, a perspective that was also not included during my tutor experience.

Overall, I think ExA has made a few good changes over the years, but there is still a lot to modify if we really want to see a change in the world through education, especially from these kind or organizations.

Final Thoughts

As we wrote above, Exa presents contradictory ideas about how to change and improve the educative system from the theory to the practise. To summarize, two main topics were addressed in our stories, ExA's education and teaching definition, and ExA's meritocratic and individual logic, both part of the ONG plan to eradicate educative inequalities. The organization selects professionals and trains them to be teachers, but expects these professionals to work at schools for only two years and then emigrate to the private sectors as leaders who can manage any situation, as the knowledge from the educational field was easily transferred to the corporative field. This situation harms the national education system because it entails several issues that need to be addressed:

- A constant mobility of teachers inside the educative system: as they ask a two-year full-life commitment, it does not seem possible for the Pexas to seriously get involved in the schools and communities they work on. Even if they decide to continue their job as teachers, it is impossible to maintain this high demand of material, physical and psychological effort.
- The low permanence of these teachers in the system makes improbable that they get involved in any kind of Union's activities, obtaining a depoliticization of the teaching activity, the role of Unions and of one of the most politicals acts: to educate.
- Constant rotation of teachers damages students who do not consolidate a trust relationship with their educator. Teachers do not usually relate with students' problems, pedagogic needs and context issues, especially in the low-income schools Pexas work, were more stability, expertise and knowledge are required. Bonding with families, schools and communities is key in teaching, and helps students and teachers to build a deeply knowledge.
- The meritocratic logic spread by ExA proposes to change students' lives through a positive attitude: if they really try, they can do anything they dream of. The "self-made-man" model does not recognize social inequality and structural problems of low income neighborhood's students as the causes of educative failure in these communities. The problem is not multidimensional addressed by this meritocratic discourse that proposes individualism as the road to global success which is contradictory.
- Pexas were not prepared to sustain the high demand of a teaching job. During the first year a quarter of selected professionals resigned ExA because they did not feel represented by the organization. Also, half of the ones who continued resigned teaching hours because of stress or the impossibility to bond with "complicated" students. Violence

between students was regular, and the lack of training of Pexas was often exposed showing that teaching was not a matter of attitude.

These points represent the most harmful results of ExA activity that constantly injure Argentinean education system. We are still convinced that educational change can be achieve, but we do not think initiatives like Teach For All are the best way to reach this objective. That is why we still work in education, with the idea that only thinking as an educative community that includes State, local and individual activities working together can achieve a substantial improvement in our national systems.It is not an easy journey and there are not short-term solutions that can be accomplished in two years, this challenge implies a strong and real compromise that is only possible to develop long term. Change is possible, but there are not magic recipes or ONG's shortcuts to success.

Note

1. If students do not pass a subject during the formal teaching period (March to December) they have two opportunities to take a test, December and February. February is the last chance of that year, that is why some students have the risk to repeat the year: to pass they must have two or fewer failed subjects' final exams.

8. "We aren't teachers, we are leaders": Situating the Teach for India Programme

VIDYA K. SUBRAMANIAN
India

Biosketch

Vidya K. Subramanian has conducted doctoral research on *Teach For India* as an instantiation of emerging public-private initiatives in education in India. Vidya's research focuses on the interaction and influence of global discourses of New Public Management upon prescriptions and practices of school reforms in India. At Tata Institute of Social Sciences, Mumbai, Vidya teaches courses on history of modern school education in India and education policy for the Masters programme in Elementary Education. Vidya's research interests include history of modern school education in South Asia, sociology of education, NGOs and development, school education policy and teacher education in South Asia.

Narrative

Introduction

> So this is actually mentioned by Wendy Kopp and Shaheen, both have mentioned it clearly that Teach for India is not a teacher developer program. It's a leadership development program. So it's job is not to train you as a teacher, its responsibility is not to train you as a teacher. And I heard a lot of criticism about that you know five weeks of Institute does not help you develop, and frankly none of us become great teachers...The idea is that two years of teaching is going to give you ground experience...what education looks like, what are the challenges, and challenges is not just pedagogy, it is about what

are the real issues in the communities, what are the real issues inside a school. So it's through teaching that you learn all these, you build leadership skills—
Raman,[1] former Teach for India Fellow (2011–2013)

After completing a post-graduate management degree from one of the most prestigious institutes in India, Raman decided to join the Teach For India (TFI) fellowship in Mumbai to understand the Indian school system. As an upper-caste[2] and upper-middle-class citizen he carried a deep dissatisfaction with his privileged schooling and professional education. In India, caste is an important socio-economic category that continues to influence how individuals access and progress through the education system. Raman believed that the TFI fellowship would finally allow him an opportunity to understand the problems within the public education system and the possibilities of reform. As the excerpt above elucidates, he didn't believe it was the objective of the programme to train teachers. It was clear that the programme aimed to create a segment of 'leaders,' individuals deeply committed to the cause of education but not to the profession of teaching.

Research on Teach For America (TFA) and some of its off-shoots have pointed to the various ways in which the programme undermines professional teacher education and institutionalises privatisation and school-choice within existing under-resourced public school systems in different parts of the world (Cumsille & Fizbein, 2015; Ellis, Maguire & Trippestad, et al., 2015; Friedrich, 2016; Straubhaar & Friedrich, 2015). This chapter maps the development of the TFI programme against the backdrop of the complex landscape of formal teacher education in India. Over the past two decades, certain landmark policies in the sphere of school education in India have paradoxically been overshadowed by the rising devolution of State[3] responsibilities of provisioning and management in education to a number of diverse private organisations (Jain, et al., 2018; Kumar, 2008, 2014; Nawani, 2002). There are four sections in this chapter. In the first section I reflect upon my research methodology. This section is significant as it outlines the difficulties of researching private initiatives working under the management of local state systems in India. I then move towards providing an overview of the formal teacher education system in the country and policy frameworks within which interventions such as TFI are increasingly seen as 'solutions' to provide 'quality' teaching to improve the academic trajectories of underprivileged students in under-resourced government schools. The third section charts the spread of the programme across the country. It briefly touches upon the pertinent differences between TFA and TFI in relation to the formal teacher education landscape and institutional structures of regulation in India. In the final section, through in-depth interviews with two cohorts of TFI Fellows,

I reconstruct key aspects of the TFI leadership model. I focus on how the programme connects school teaching to building leadership, which is increasingly being seen as the panacea for education reform.

Researching Private Interventions: Field-Work and Methods Employed

As of 2015, TFI had 1,084 Fellows enrolled and teaching close to 60,000 students across a segment of government and private schools in Mumbai, Pune, Delhi, Chennai, Hyderabad, Bangalore and Ahmedabad (Teach For India website: www.teachforindia.org). The programme operated in 320 government, government-aided and privately managed schools across these seven cities. What is important to note is that while the intervention operated in less than two-percent of the total number of government and private schools across the country, it is emerging as a focal point in a growing network of urban not-for-profit organisations advocating for privatisation and school-choice as key measures to reform the ailing public school system in India (Subramanian, 2018).

This chapter draws on my Ph.D. research study that focused on a case-study of the TFI programme in Delhi. Of all the cities where the programme functions, it is in Delhi that TFI recruits the largest number of Fellows to teach in a segment of government and low-income[4] private schools (Subramanian, 2017). Around 285 TFI Fellows worked in 67 government schools (of the total 2817 government schools) and 14 privately managed schools in the city.

I examined the intervention within larger discourses of New Public Management (NPM) that are entering school systems in the country and are actively promoted as measures to resurrect 'inefficient' government schools (Clarke, Gewirtz, & McLaughlin, 2000; Jain, Mehendale, Mukhopadhyay, et al., 2018). On reviewing research on the TFA programme and a few of its off-shoots in the U.K., Australia, and South America (Blandford, 2014; Brewer & deMarrais, 2015; Cumsille & Fizbein, 2015; Skourdoumbis, 2012; Straubhaar & Friedrich, 2015), I noted that most of the scholarship on the internal dynamics of the programme has been conducted by former Corps Members/Fellows, apart from some noted education research scholars based in these respective countries. This indicates that the programme in the Western[5] context has an interface with existing formal teacher education systems and provides certain pathways that allow Fellows to engage with this space academically thus allowing for some conversations around education and linking it to a larger politics of social justice, class and equity (Crawford-Garrett, 2012). Critiques emerging from TFA Alumni have also opened up important debates on not just the complexities and struggles of teaching but also the politics through which the organization keeps dissenting voices out of mainstream education discourses (Brewer & deMarrais, 2015). These studies are noteworthy for they provide some important background to situate and compare the intervention's Indian off-shoot and understand how academic research on private interventions in India is hindered by the State itself.

I conducted research on TFI as a Ph.D. student based in one of India's foremost public universities[6] in Delhi. My fieldwork spanned from July 2014 to October 2015. After conducting a brief series of pilot interviews with a few TFI Fellows in Delhi, who I came to be acquainted with through a former TFI colleague, I approached the TFI Delhi city team to enquire about the possibilities of conducting research on the intervention in the city. My proposal was met with hesitation[7] and I was asked to seek formal permission from the regional wings of the Municipal Corporation of Delhi (MCD), the local government body, that manages the largest number of primary schools in the city. I was denied permission by the MCD. Researchers are often seen with much suspicion by government officials and considering the strict regulations of local state control across government schools in the city, navigating school sites without formal permission is a difficult affair. As I was denied official permission by TFI and the MCD, I enquired about possibilities of volunteering with some TFI Fellows I had befriended. Through them, I was given an opportunity at a school site not far from where I resided. I worked as a volunteer assisting the TFI Fellow in her classroom activities for three months before I was asked to leave due to the existing tensions at the school site between the government staff and the TFI Fellows.

Considering the difficult nature of accessing and studying the intervention within government schools, I followed up on my brief period of volunteering with TFI with in-depth interviews with TFI Fellows and TFI organisation members. Close to 40 detailed interviews were conducted with TFI members largely based in Delhi and others based in the cities of Mumbai, Pune, Hyderabad, Bangalore, Chennai and Ahmedabad between September 2014 and October 2015. During the course of my interviews, I also requested the respondents to share literature they received from the organization during their five-week training module and on other aspects that outline TFI's vision for education reform. None of the members interviewed had any organised literature or resources from their training module.[8] I received two important reports from a TFI Fellow which were significant in understanding TFI's long-term vision of reform for the Indian education system.

Apart from in-depth interviews, Right to Information[9] (RTI) applications were also filed at respective Delhi government offices to procure relevant information on the PPP arrangement between TFI and the Delhi government. The RTI responses provided me with important information on the terms of the Memorandum of Understanding (MOU) between TFI and the Delhi government as well as data on the spread of the programme in the city. I analysed information and narratives from these various sources to understand the organisation's vision of education reform and its modalities of functioning within government schools in Delhi.

Fragmented and Under-Resourced Terrain of Teacher Education in India

The history of modern school education in India is inextricably linked to its colonial past. Before the British began to rule parts of India in the late eighteenth century, the school teacher within the diverse South Asian context was embedded within differing social and religious norms. There were vast differences with regard to the forms of schooling, the codes and media of instruction, curriculum and the purposes of education. These variations were further complicated by issues of caste, social class, and gender that privileged formal modes of learning largely among upper-castes. The existing diverse indigenous systems of teaching and learning underwent much change once these institutions came under colonial control and the school teacher became a functionary of the colonial Indian State earning a meagre salary (Kumar, 1991; Rao, 2014).

Post-independence, elementary education in India was envisaged as a key institution through which "equality of opportunity and social justice could be achieved" (Nambissan & Rao, 2013). The Indian State's engagement in the realm of elementary education has differed across the decades. Where in the 1950s elementary education lost out to greater investment in science, technology, and higher education, it was only with the Kothari Commission Report in 1964, that it re-entered public discussion forcefully (Batra, 2012).

There were wide variations across India with regard to duration of teacher training, course curriculum, as well as age and educational requirements for entry into teacher education institutes. Up to the 1970s, education was largely the responsibility of regional state governments in India and training of school teachers largely took place in stand-alone teacher education institutes outside the purview and regulation of the University system (Batra, 2006, 2012; Khora, 2011).

The late 1980s and 1990s saw the opening up of the economy and implementation of structural adjustment programmes that severely restricted the Indian State from spending on the social sector, largely education and health. Foreign aid mediated the Indian state's efforts in education reform during this period. During this phase, the role of the school teacher and the profession of school teaching gained some importance. However, the Indian state's cut-back on social spending had repercussions on reforming teacher education as well.

The mass scale expansion of the school education system during the 1990s brought people from a variety of socio-economic backgrounds into the teaching profession. There was much concern about the failing standards of teacher training as was highlighted by the Chattopadhyay Commission Report (1983–1985) which called for reforming teacher education programmes institutionally. It emphasised the need to locate teacher education within the University system in order to bring more depth and rigour to the training programmes (Batra, 2006; Govinda, 2002).

Despite these disparate efforts at the national level to formulate policy frameworks and quality norms, it was largely up to the regional state governments to decide on conditions concerning teacher recruitment. This exacerbated existing variations in teaching standards across the country (Govinda & Josephine, 2005). Instead of filling up the several vacancies for school teachers across states in the country, most states took the economically viable route out by appointing contract teachers under various schemes. These stop-gap measures at the local level diluted the quality of teacher education further.

The 1980s saw a diverse group of autonomous organisations broadly categorised under the umbrella term of non-governmental organisations (NGOs) come into being as an active response to the inefficiency of the Indian State across a range of issues encompassing human rights, environment, development, gender and education (Katzenstein, Kothari, & Mehta, 2001). These NGOs were distinct from conventional voluntary organisations aimed at charity and inscribed within religion and altruism (Kamat, 2002; Nawani, 2002). The engagements between the Indian State and these diverse private entities became the precursor to Public-Private Partnerships (PPPs), a term that gained much traction through the twenty-first century in Indian education policy documents.

The twenty-first century brought a series of landmark policy reforms in the field of elementary education that sought to make the Indian State more accountable to its vast population of children enrolled in a range of government schools across the country. Discussions on curriculum and free and compulsory education for all children up to the age of 14 came into the public domain with the National Curriculum Framework, 2005 (NCF) and the Right to Education Act, 2009 (RTE). The NCF, 2005, was a commendable accomplishment that sought to strengthen the idea of developing a more child-centred pedagogical approach that connected curriculum to the diverse social realities of the child.[10] Through the NCF 2005, the task of the school teacher gained more importance as she was seen as a central agent in facilitating the process of child-centred learning within the classroom (Batra, 2006, 2012).

The Right to Education Act 2009 stipulated strong quality guidelines on teacher education. This landmark policy measure that made the Indian State finally accountable to provide free and compulsory education to all children up to the age of 14 dramatically increased student enrolment making teacher scarcity in the school system more apparent. As of 2014, there was a shortage of 940,000 teachers in government schools in the country. This included 586,000 teachers in primary schools and 350,000 lakh teachers in upper primary schools. In addition, around 600,000 teachers remain untrained.[11] These inadequacies also reflected the decreasing financial support of the Indian State to the public school system. The ratio of public education expenditure to the Gross Domestic Product (GDP) has steadily declined from a peak of 4.4% in 1989 to 3.6% or so towards the end of the decade (Sen & Dreze, 2003). With regard to teacher education specifically, Batra (2012) underscores the proliferation of sub-standard teacher education institutions in the past two decades post the neo-liberal reforms. More than 80% of teacher education institutions in India are managed by a highly unregulated private sector.

Paradoxically, these progressive policies have also been contradicted through an increasing reliance on partnerships with a range of private entities to improve quality of education within the public school system. The Indian state's role has been dramatically reduced and service delivery functions are increasingly being outsourced to diverse NGOs. While some prominent corporates have run charitable foundations for a range of social issues including education, contributed towards welfare measures in limited capacities and funded select NGOs over the years in India, this move signified an expanded role for global and Indian corporates in participating in Public-Private Partnerships to reform school education (Sundar, 2013).

Teach For India: Reorienting Teaching in Urban Public School Systems

The entry of TFI into the urban public-school system in India is linked to the corporate NGO networks functioning in the top-tier cities (Subramanian, 2018). In Mumbai, where the programme was initiated, a number of NGOs were already working in differing capacities to reform the under-resourced and poorly functioning urban public schooling system in the city through the 1990s (Subramanian, 2018). One such NGO was the Akanksha Foundation, whose founder Shaheen Mistri was instrumental in moulding the TFI programme as an effective alternative to bring in quality education into a segment of government and low-income schools that catered to underprivileged children in Mumbai (Vellanki, 2014). Like TFI, Akanksha Foundation also worked on a model of volunteer-teachers who had no formal exposure to teacher education apart from short training sessions in the foundation's in-house modules of literacy and numeracy (Gupta & Mistri, 2014; Vellanki, 2014).

As the Akanksha Foundation was working in select capacities within government and low-income schools in Mumbai and Pune, Shaheen Mistri was also keen to find opportunities that would help her expand the scope of her organisation. She became acquainted with Wendy Kopp, founder of TFA in 2007. The idea of mobilising college students as agents of change within the education sector drew on Shaheen Mistri's own experiences of setting up the Akanksha Foundation. Through collaborations with a range of Indian and global organizations: Archana Patel and Anand Patel (Indicorps), Anand Shah (Piramal Enterprises), Nandita Dugar (Boston Consulting Group), Anu Aga (TSIF), Bill and Melinda Gates Foundation and Vandana Goyal (who was with McKinsey Global Management Consulting Group at that time), a blueprint for the Teach For India fellowship was developed (Gupta & Mistri 2014, p. 72). Teach For India was officially launched in 2009 in Mumbai and Pune. The programme selected 87 Fellows to work in a segment of municipal and low-income private schools in these cities (Gupta & Mistri, 2014; Subramanian, 2018; Vellanki, 2014).

One of the key differences between the TFA model and TFI was that the former programme came into being within larger policy developments in the U.S. that created a space for Alternative Teaching Certification (ATC) routes (Hohnstein, 2008; Maloney, 2012). In TFA, it is mandatory for Corps Members (as the participants of the programme are called) to be enrolled in an accredited formal teacher education program during the course of their two-year fellowship. This meant that Corps Members had to complete certain formal requirements of teacher education apart from the organisation's five-week training programme as well. Increasingly, TFA in conjunction with the Relay Graduate School has started to isolate the formalised teacher training as a largely in-house process. There are several critiques to how ATC courses dilute formal teacher education programmes and focus only on practice-oriented concerns in pedagogy as opposed to more theoretical, historical, and philosophical foundations of teacher education (Hohnstein, 2008; Labaree, 2010). Keeping these limitations of ATCs in mind, it is important to note that TFA still operates within a formal apparatus of teacher education in the U.S.

In India, however, TFI remains outside the purview of the formal teacher education system. Fellows receive training and mentorship exclusively from the TFI organisation before being placed to teach in government and low-income schools. While teacher education regulations enshrined in the RTE (2009) mandate that only those with recognized diplomas or under-graduate degrees in education could teach in government schools, TFI operates through certain local government PPPs that allow much leeway to NGOs to work outside these policy guidelines. These freedoms indicate measures by tiers of the Indian State to allow for privatisation and in turn compromise on State investment in formal teacher education (Mehendale & Mukhopadhyay, 2018; Subramanian, 2017).

Considering the programme's close connections with TFA, curricular objectives of the model were also a significant sphere of contention. When TFI first began its programme in Mumbai schools in mid 2009, the organisation's curricular objectives for English and mathematics were aligned to the U.S. Common Core standards.[12] In Mumbai, Fellows utilised texts and resources largely utilised in U.S. classrooms. However, the expansion of the programme over the past decade has also resulted in the organisation making some cursory attempts to adopt Indian national curricular norms for teaching (Subramanian, 2017). The move to enter municipal schools in cities falling within different federal and linguistic geographies of the country has also led the intervention to make some attempts to map its curricular objectives onto state curricular standards.[13]

The profile of TFI Fellows was similar in many ways to the TFA programme. Most candidates came from privileged middle class and upper-caste backgrounds who had completed their under-graduate and post-graduate education from prestigious educational institutions in prime cities across the country (Subramanian, 2017). Close to 50% of the applicants were mid-career professionals from technical and corporate management backgrounds looking to shift into careers in the social sector. Around 40% of the applicants were university graduates keen to experience volunteerism. None of the applicants, however, were individuals with an under-graduate degree in education or looking for a career as a school teacher.[14] There are several institutional reasons linked to the education bureaucracy and administration that limited TFI Fellows entry into school-teaching in India but most importantly the Fellowship's central focus on leadership markets the programme exclusively as an aspirational forum for budding social sector 'managers.'

Contrary to the transition in the U.S., where TFA began as an organisation seeking to fill teacher shortages starting in 1990, TFI posited itself largely as a programme geared to build 'leadership' among its Fellows (Scott,

Trujillo & Rivera, 2016; Subramanian, 2017). This can be seen in the organisation's vision of a 'long-term theory of change'. The thrust of the 'long term theory of change' meant that through the experience of the two-year fellowship, Fellows would be motivated to consider options which saw them working to achieve 'education equity' largely *outside* the public school system (Teach For India, 2014, p. 6). There were significant differences between the post-fellowship trajectories of TFA Fellows and TFI Fellows.

An internal report by the organization noted that "while the overall percentage of TFA and TFI Alumni working full-time in education is not very different (between 60% and 65% for both organizations), the split by role/pathway in education is striking in its contrast" (Teach For India, 2015, p. 8). Where in TFA, some alumni members did take up roles within the public school system after the completion of their fellowship, in TFI this engagement with the government system was negligible. More than 90% of TFI Fellows ended up taking roles only in education and development organisations in the private sector (Ibid).

The report showed that of the 11,000 alumni members of TFA (as of 2015) who continued to work as school teachers, nearly 48% worked in district public schools as teachers. This number must also be seen in terms of the entire TFA alumni network totaling more than 50,000 members at the time. In comparison, of the 1,050 alumni members of TFI, only 70 Alumni members (6.7% of the total Alumni members) continued to work as school teachers. What was interesting to note was that none of these 70 TFI Alumni members worked in government schools. All of them worked "either in high-fee private schools or schools run by nonprofit organizations, some of which have a partnership with the government" (Ibid).

The report also pointed to notable differences between the post-fellowship trajectories of TFI and TFA Fellows in school administration and management roles. It showed that in the U.S., approximately 250 TFA alumni members worked as 'school-system leaders.' They served as superintendents in several public school districts. In contrast, such roles did not exist for TFI Alumni members in the Indian context. This indicated differences not only in the administrative and bureaucratic structures between both countries, but also suggested deeper structural separations between civil society engagements with the formal government apparatus (Mukhopadhyay, 2011; Teach For India, 2015).[15]

The vast majority of TFI Fellows—more than 70%—worked within nonprofit organisations. The report highlighted information from internal surveys that showed that most TFI Fellows had a preference for roles in the private sector through the CSR divisions of corporate companies. When probed on the underlying disinclination to work full-time in the public education system, reasons pointed to the vast differences in pay scales between corporate and social sectors, lack of career growth options and placements in areas far away from major cities (Ibid).

Where on the one hand, TFI sought to work towards 'education equity' and bringing quality education to the poor child in under resourced schools, the future aspirations of those who enter the organisation dominated its frame of reference. The complex pedagogical labour of school teaching, most notably, found no place in its leadership framework.

From 'Teaching as Leadership' to the 'Leadership Development Journey'

The TFI training module, like its American counterpart, takes place over a period of five weeks and provided a hands-on introduction to Fellows on the organisation's frameworks, processes of teaching, and structures of mentorship in practice. Until 2014, the guiding framework of TFI was based on the U.S. Teaching as Leadership (TAL) model developed by TFA. The TAL model, was an extensively detailed framework that focused on six prominent pillars of teacher action: (1) setting big goals; (2) investing students and others; (3) planning purposefully; (4) executing effectively; (5) continuously increasing effectiveness; and (6) working relentlessly. These teacher actions were mapped onto a gradation of teacher proficiency, moving from pre-novice to exemplary. The model broke down teaching processes into several micro levels and the primary focus was on the Fellow steering students towards pre-decided learning outcomes.

However, in 2014, TFI developed its own guiding framework called the Leadership Development Journey (LDJ). While inspired by the TAL rubric, the content and underpinning of this framework was significantly different. Unlike the TAL, which was close to a 20-page document, the LDJ was a two-page document comprising of two important scales which complemented each other: (1) the Student Vision Scale (SVS); and (2) the Fellow Commitments Scale (FCS). There were three strands within each of these scales moving from a point scale of one which was the lowest to five which was the highest. The SVS included academic achievement, values and mindsets, and access and exposure, while the FCS included commitment to personal transformation, commitment to collective action and commitment to education equity.

The underlying focus of the SVS was a simple gradation that sought to connect the Fellows' efforts as a teacher with the behaviour and learning outcomes of her students. Unlike the TAL, the SVS transitioned from a general premise of children being destructive or not learning towards becoming independent and joyful learners. The scale did not elaborate on what these attributes meant in detail and the discretion of judgement was left to the Program Manager who used this scale to assess the Fellows who were under her supervision as they taught in government and low-income schools through the course of two years.

The SVS was linked to the FCS in pertinent ways. The FCS saw the Fellow as an individual whose work was to extend beyond the classroom (as defined by the SVS) and connect several concentric eco-systems: the classroom, the school and the community. As Chandni, a Fellow from the 2014 to 2016 cohort explained:

> So there are two things that are the centre of the LDJ. First of all the leader which is you, and the people you are leading, that is your kids. As far as the kids go so a person who is a true leader has to take into account the most important things that affect the life of the people you are leading right. So obviously in the Indian scenario, or any other scenario, the people that would come into the ambit of the students' lives would be the people in the school, the administrators, the teachers and their community and parents, their family. Especially the community in which we work in, like because of their special challenges, the economic challenges, the social challenges, the educational challenges, there are so many influences in these kids' lives, so it is not just explaining to them content from books or values, just saying that okay this is respect, because they see just the opposite of that happening in their community or sometimes in the schools. So to teach respect to the kids and then to challenge what they already know that is existing in the school and in the community, I think that is what leadership is all about.

The Fellow's role was not just teaching, as Chandni elaborated. It was to create conditions of 'leadership' as well. How Fellows understood this rubric and put into practice their various teaching strategies was influenced by a host of factors. Within the space of the classroom the teaching practices of the Fellows were influenced by their personal dispositions regarding school teaching, TFI's training and mentorship requirements as well as the dynamics of the government school system.

None of the Fellows interviewed viewed the fellowship as an opportunity to enter teaching as a vocation. All Fellows noted that two years were not enough to be a good teacher. They clearly distinguished their profile of work within the two-year fellowship from the long-term vocation of teaching associated with government school teachers.

Fellows understood their engagement with practices of teaching, building relationships with government school staff, children and their families within the framework of 'leadership.' Vineet described what he understood of the programme's thrust of relating teaching with 'leadership':

> I don't think there are any rules in Teach for India [...] And that's the beauty and the sad part about it is that you get to define what is leadership and what is teacher for you, you have to define everything, no body can force you to do anything. There is no way that anyone can make you do anything here. And that is the system that you are given a support system, the process of getting into it is such that at least you are mildly passionate about it [...] and then they expect you to create your own definition [...] you are just taking in, what is happening in the world, and you are trying to form definition of what exactly a leader is.

His observation highlighted the ambiguity within the programme in linking teaching with 'leadership.' The organisation provided Fellows with a broad support system. However, it was up to the Fellows to explore and define the processes in their own individual way. The rubric did not define any specific criteria but Fellows' practices in the classroom suggested that the organisation valued structures of classroom management, codes of discipline and English language reading and writing skills. Teaching processes were heavily biased towards the TFI framework of literacy and numeracy which was in turn linked to standardised testing.

However, the space of the classroom was largely seen as a beginning, an engagement which had limited 'impact.' Ravi noted the limitations of just focusing on the classroom:

> I think most of the Fellows, when they think about their future, they don't want to restrict themselves to 40 kids or 50 kids. Because for me, like I know that if I want to do something more, why not create a system or a structure where through me more and more students and I just don't become the foot soldier of an army like Teach for India, and why not I just build my own movement where I am impacting more classroom, more community, more lives.

For him, the classroom was a finite space and he aspired for more. He hoped to build a system where he could work with a greater number of people, 'impacting' more classrooms and more communities. This meant building relationships with different stakeholders in the school system and the community and to work towards 'education equity.' Again, like 'leadership,' 'education equity' was not clearly defined by the organisation. It was left to Fellows to interpret this construct in their own individualised ways and to do what they could to achieve 'education equity' within the school site they worked in.

To achieve 'education equity,' Fellows implemented diverse projects within their classrooms, schools, and communities. They raised funds through their personal and professional networks specifically for their classrooms within the government or low-income school. These measures also created tension and inequities in resources between TFI classrooms and other school teachers' classrooms (Subramanian, 2017).

The initiatives that TFI Fellows undertook were inextricably connected to how they were evaluated by their Program Managers on the FCS. The process of gathering 'evidence' in the classroom and through other activities suggested certain complex concerns. Neeraj discussed the negotiations involved in the process of gathering and substantiating 'evidences':

> The problem is elsewhere, which is the evidences if you admit the wide range, the anecdotes, something which the child wrote, something which happened, is easy to, there are Fellows who go with all these evidences also, and at the same time their classroom may not be what their evidences claim. Just because a child one day wrote this doesn't mean this value is instilled in him. And these are very rough evidences, they have no credibility at all, you may just pile up such evidences which are available very cheaply if you are only out looking for them. And of course you only choose to report the positive things which you saw, because they are the ones the PM [Program Manager] is interested in.

His observation pointed to a lack of pedagogical grounding in how Fellows understood 'evidences' and why they collected it. Neeraj's comment also alluded to how Fellows involved themselves in numerous activities to showcase 'evidences' in order to secure a positive evaluation from the Program Manager on the FCS. There was a lack of effort in engaging with substantial dimensions of what constructs like 'leadership' or 'education equity' meant in the context of a poorly functioning public school system.

The school system with its bureaucratic structure, administrative hierarchies, and modes of teaching-learning within school sites and the myriad complex engagements and relationships between various stakeholders, were imagined as mechanical parts of a whole. Each Fellow could engage with different facets of this system in their own ways to bring about 'change'. These templates of 'leadership' were driven by a sense of 'individual entrepreneurialism' (Gooptu, 2009, p. 45). Gooptu's (2009) study on deciphering the new 'enterprising' self-identity among retail sector workers in the eastern urban region of India is of significance here in situating Fellows narratives of 'leadership'. She noted that with the transition of the Indian State from an interventionist to a regulatory state encouraging of market and business friendly policies, "new workplaces like organised retail shopping malls are playing a decisive part in crafting suitable workers and citizens, and in re-shaping individual subjectivity, consonant with the needs of the market and neoliberal governmentality for self-governing citizens and self-driven, pliant workers" (Ibid: 54). Workers were not only socialised into values of 'personal initiative,' 'enterprise,' 'hard work,' 'individual responsibility' and 'self-discipline' but also learnt to seek "personal solutions to structurally or systematically generated problems in the economy and at the workplace" (Ibid). It was in this similar vein of 'enterprise culture,' that Fellows began to view themselves as individual 'change agents' developing 'personal solutions' to reform the education system.

The larger idea of this intervention was to support individuals in discovering their own narratives of 'change' through the course of engaging with underprivileged children. Most Fellows' post-fellowship professional choices were to remain within the education sector either through working with NGOs, research consultancies, joining senior staff positions in TFI or applying for CSR foundations of corporates that had a strong focus on education.

There was only one Fellow, Amit, in my sample of respondents who was looking to pursue the unconventional route of studying a Masters in Sociology at Delhi University. His choice was considered radical among his peers but Amit's choice was driven by a range of reasons:

> I would say that the Fellowship has given me a path and sort of a vague definition of where do I fit in, in trying to fulfil what needs to be done. Having said that, is education that path, I'm not necessarily sure. Because I am, after coming into the Fellowship I've realized, that even the government has certain handicaps, like they are also thinking at some level, they are also thinking of learning outcomes, they are also thinking of education in terms of learning outcomes. So they are coming with certain assumptions. They are putting a certain kind of life upon us. Now whether I am even comfortable with that sort of life, I'm not sure with that idea. [...] And that is why I want to get into Sociology to kind of think through what others have thought through.

He believed that while the fellowship provided him with the opportunity to engage with the education system, he was not completely sure if the organisation's path of education reform was something he subscribed to. Amit realised that while TFI was influential in pushing for certain kinds of teaching and testing practices within school sites, he also saw that these measures were not operating within a vacuum. The Indian government too, according to him, was supporting and encouraging of these measures. Amit's observation was pertinent because it articulated a sense of scepticism and need to engage with larger systems of knowledge to understand these complexities. This was a contrast to most Fellows who believed that their two-year experience had equipped them with enough knowledge on the education system and the pathways to institute 'change'.

His comment also signified the tensions within various levels of the public education system as well. At the level of national policy, guidelines of the

National Curricular Framework (2005) and the Right To Education (2009) sought to reform several dimensions of teaching-learning within the school. This included curricular reforms to focus on a more child-centred approach to teaching, bringing more autonomy to the school teacher and changing the examination system to a process of continuous evaluation through multiple modes. However, at the level of the local government school, these policy prescriptions towards reforming the system were often side-lined and rarely implemented in practice. Interventions such as TFI were thus operating within lacunae that the Indian State had institutionalised within the landscape of teacher education and public schooling post-independence and which had, in turn, deteriorated post the neoliberal reforms in the 1990s.

Conclusions

In India, the formal terrain of teacher education and public school education has historically seen a poor involvement by the State—both at the national and at the regional levels. The fragmented landscape of public school education was further impacted through the 1990s as the Indian State devolved tasks of provision and delivery to a diverse range of NGOs, some of which were concentrated in niche urban geographies and supported by corporate entities with limited ideas of education reform. TFI was one such corporate-backed intervention that advocated leadership as a solution to poorly trained teachers in a segment of under resourced urban public schools catering to underprivileged children. The programme had no interface with formal institutions of teacher education in the country. This is unlike several "Teach for ..." off-shoots that are mandated to function within certain regulations of formal teacher education in their respective countries. The division of public and private was even more stark in the context of TFI and TFA as in the Indian context Fellows gravitated to largely working within non-profit education organisations run by corporates and few sought to engage with the government sector. Unlike TFA where the programme initially did seek to develop a framework of school teaching, even if drawing from pedagogical ideas of behaviourism, TFI evolved its model largely within discourses of leadership. These discourses were often narrow and geared towards Fellows' own individual visions of education reform with little understanding of what their engagements would mean in the context of a much-ignored public education system and larger ideas of education equity. 'Leadership' thus emerged as an important catch-word for all kinds of experiences and activities conducted through the course of the two-year fellowship that the Fellow could showcase as significant contributions that would benefit her outside the public school system and with little or no constructive pedagogical outcome for the students concerned.

Notes

1. Names of all respondents are anonymous to maintain confidentiality.
2. Caste has a long and complex history in the Indian context. Historically education has been the reserve only of upper-castes, most notably Brahmins (those born into the priestly caste), in India. Through the colonial period there have been important struggles by lower-castes to access education and employment. India gained Independence in 1947 and the Indian Constitution has several provisions for the social upliftment of marginalized sections in the country. However, despite some development in various arenas post-Independence, caste continues to play an important role in education and social mobility in India even today. This chapter does not seek to interrogate caste privileges among TFI Fellows specifically but it is necessary to acknowledge that like Teach for America (which has changed marginally today as individuals from minority communities do enter the programme), TFI attracts individuals largely from a certain segment of privileged social, educational and professional backgrounds (For varied discussions on caste and education in India see: Bhattacharya, 2002; Jodhka, 2012).
3. In this chapter State, government and public schooling will be used interchangeably to refer to schools that are administered by the Indian State. That is these schools receive funding, support and are regulated by a combination of municipal, state and central government administrative bodies. India is a federal union of 29 states and 7 union territories. Teach for India, at present, operates across seven cities in the country that are a part of different states with diverse linguistic, social and regional histories.
4. Low-cost or low-income private or budget schools operate with a minimum of infrastructure and resources. Teachers in these schools are largely unqualified and are paid a fraction of what tenured teachers receive in government schools (Nambissan, 2012).
5. I use Western here largely to refer to Anglophone countries such as the US, UK and Australia. The bulk of scholarship on the Teach for programmes comes from these regions based on my literature review for my Ph.D. study.
6. I was based at the Zakir Husain Centre for Educational Studies in Jawaharlal Nehru University (JNU), Delhi. As a Central University it receives funding from the Central government.
7. The Head Office of TFI based in Mumbai had given permission to a research team from the School of International and Public Affairs, Columbia University, to conduct a longitudinal study on the programme sometime in 2010–2011. Details of this study were not shared with me. A search on the internet led me to a cursory report published in April 2012 (Measuring Effectiveness and Impact of the Teach for India programme). The methodology largely seeks to compare the programme vis a vis government school teachers to showcase that TFI is a better alternative. The comparison and results are sketchy.
8. TFI Fellows provided me with access to an online drive where a range of resources for teaching Literacy and Maths modules were uploaded. Upon going through the drive, I found that there were no critical pedagogical underpinnings to how or why these resources were organised in certain ways. Most of the resources, interestingly, were links to American websites that advocated standardised learning and testing. The 'selling-point' of these resources was that these were practices that worked in the classroom and led to 'learning outcomes'. My PhD study showed that even though TFI

followed a behaviourist framework drawing from Benjamin Bloom's ideas of learning, none of the TFI Fellows had any in-depth engagement with this realm of academic literature as well. Most TFI Fellows had a shallow engagement with behaviourist models of learning as well and most of them had never engaged with any critical pedagogical literature that questioned behaviourism.

9. The Right to Information is an Act passed by the Indian Parliament in 2005 that mandates timely responses to citizen requests for government information (https://rti.gov.in). The Act, despite certain limitations, seeks to empower citizens, promote transparency and accountability in the functioning of the government. In the context of this research study, the RTI was an important tool for the researcher to gain information on MoUs between private organisations and the government that are not shared on the public forum.
10. Before the NCF 2005, there were very few spaces in the Indian education system where child-centred pedagogical methods were valued and given the due they deserved. Teaching-learning processes in the Indian school system have largely been dominated by rote learning methods that favour memorisation and cramming of facts.
11. This data was part of the report on the status and challenges of the RTE authored by Ambarish Rai, Convener of the Right to Education Forum, published on the Common Causes website (http://www.commoncause.in/publication_details.php?id=466) on October-December 2015.
12. The Common Core State Standards Initiative is an educational initiative in the United States that details what students from Grade 1 to 12 should know in English and Maths at the end of each grade. The initiative seeks to establish consistent educational standards across the states in the US and ensure that students graduating from high school are prepared to join college programmes or the workforce (Common Core standards website: www.corestandards.org).
13. These guidelines however do not hold strongly within private low-income schools where the intervention also works. Information from interviews with respective City Team members.
14. Information gathered through in-depth interviews with Public Relations Head of the national TFI team based in Mumbai in 2015.
15. The role of a district superintendent in the US context, according to the report, was equivalent to the position of an Education Officer in a local municipal government. In the Indian bureaucratic system, these roles are traditionally occupied by individuals from the state or central civil services. The entry to the state and central civil services in India involves passing through several levels of centralized examinations and interviews before being selected to serve as a civil servant. Thus deeper systemic administrative structures separated civil society intervention within the formal government space in the Indian context vis a vis the American context.

References

Batra, P. (2012). Positioning teachers in the emerging education landscape of contemporary India. *India Infrastructure Report 2012: Private Sector in Education*. New Delhi: Routledge, 219–231.

Batra, P. (2006). Building on the national curriculum framework to enable the agency of teachers. *Contemporary Education Dialogue*, *4*(1), 88–118.

Bhattacharya, S. (Ed.). (2002). *Education and the disprivileged: Nineteenth and twentieth century India*. New Delhi: Orient Longman.

Blandford, S. (2014). Leading through partnership: Enhancing the Teach First leadership programme. *Teacher Development: An International Journal of Teachers' Professional Development, 18*(1), 1–14.

Brewer, T. J. & deMarrais, K. (Eds.). (2015). *Teach for America counter narratives: Alumni speak up and speak out*. New York: Peter Lang Publishing.

Clarke, J., Gewirtz, S., & McLaughlin, E. (Eds.). (2000). *New managerialism, new welfare?* London: Thousand Oaks.

Crawford-Garrett, K. (2012). *Teacher literacies in the age of reform: Teach for America, urban schooling and the methods course as a site for productive disruption* (Doctoral Dissertation). Available from ProQuest Dissertations and Theses database. (UMI Number: 3510992)

Cumsille R, B. & Fizbein, A. (2015). Crème de la crème: The Teach for All experience and its lessons for policy making in Latin America. *Education Policy Analysis Archives, 23*(46), 1–26.

Dreze, J. & Sen, A. (2003). Basic education as a political issue. In J.B.G. Tilak (Ed.) *Education, society and development: National and international perspectives*. New Delhi: NIEPA.

Ellis, V., Maguire, M. Trippestad, T., et al. (2015). Teaching other people's children, elsewhere, for a while: The rhetoric of a travelling education reform. *Journal of Education Policy*, 1–21.

Friedrich, D. (2016). Teach for All, public-private partnerships, and the erosion of the public in education. In A. Verger, C. Lubienski, & G. Steiner-Khamsi (Eds.), *World yearbook of education 2016: The global education industry* (pp. 160–174). New York: Routledge.

Gooptu, N. (2009). Neoliberal subjectivity, enterprise culture and new workplaces: Organised retail and shopping malls in India. *Economic and Political Weekly, 44*(22), 45–54.

Govinda, R. (2002). *India education report*. New Delhi: Oxford University Press.

Govinda, R. & Josephine, Y. (2005). Para-teachers in India: A Review. *Contemporary Education Dialogue*, Spring, *2*(2), 193–224.

Gupta, K. & Mistri, S. (2014). *Redrawing India: The Teach for India story*. Gurgaon: Random House Publishers India Pvt. Ltd.

Hohnstein, S. (2008). *The rise of alternative teaching certification in relation to students who are impoverished, ethnic minorities and change in teacher salary in United States public schools* (Doctoral dissertation). Available from ProQuest Dissertations and Theses database. (UMI No. 3307336).

Jain, M., Mehendale, A., Mukhopadhyay, R., Sarangapani, P., & Winch, C. (Eds.). (2018). *School education in India: Market, state and quality*. London and New York: Routledge.

Jodhka, S. (2012). *Caste: Oxford India short introductions*. New Delhi: Oxford University Press.

Kamat, S. (2002). *Development hegemony: NGOs and the state in India.* New Delhi: Oxford University Press.

Katzenstein, M., Kothari, S., & Mehta, U. (2001). Social movement politics in india: Institutions, interests, and identities. In A. Kohli (Ed.), *The success of india's democracy* (pp. 242–269). Cambridge: Cambridge University Press.

Khora, S. (2011). *Education and teacher professionalism: Study of teachers and classroom processes.* Jaipur and New Delhi: Rawat Publications.

Kumar, K. (1991). *Political agenda of education: A study of colonialist and nationalist ideas.* New Delhi: Sage Publications.

Kumar, K. (2008). Partners in education? *Economic and Political Weekly, XLIII*(3), 8–11.

Kumar, M. (2014). Law, statistics, public-private partnership and emergence of a new Subject. Retrieved March 18, 2019 from http://www.mcrg.ac.in/PP67.pdf

Labaree, D. (2010). Teach For America and teacher ed: Heads they win, tails we lose. *Journal of Teacher Education, 61*(1–2), 48–55.

Maloney, P. A. (2012). *Schools make teachers: The case of Teach For America and teacher training* (Doctoral dissertation). Available from ProQuest Dissertations and Theses database. (UMI No. 3525331).

Mehendale, A. & Mukhopadhyay, R. (2018). Regulatory state and the diversified private. In M. Jain, Mehendale, A., Mukhopadhyay, R., Sarangapani, P., & Winch, C. (Eds.) *School education in India: Market, state and quality.* London and New York: Routledge.

Mukhopadhyay, R. (2011). *Anthropology of the education bureaucracy.* (Unpublished doctoral dissertation). National Institute of Advanced Studies, Bangalore.

Nambissan, G. (2012). Private schools for the poor: Business as usual? *Economic and Political Weekly, XLVII*(41), 51–58

Nambissan, G. & Rao, S. (2013). *Sociology of education in India: Changing contours and emerging concerns.* New Delhi: Oxford University Press.

Nawani, D. (2002). Role and contribution of non-governmental organizations in basic education. In R. Govinda (Ed.) *India education report.* New Delhi: Oxford University Press, pp. 121–130.

Rao, P (Ed.). (2014). *New perspectives in the history of Indian education.* New Delhi: Orient Blackswan.

Scott, J., Trujillo, T. & Rivera, M. D. (2016). Reframing Teach For America: A conceptual framework for the next generation of scholarship. *Education Policy Analysis Archives, 24*(12), 1–28.

Skourdoumbis, A. (2012). Teach For Australia (TFA): Can it overcome educational disadvantage? *Asia Pacific Journal of Education, 32*(3), 305–315.

Straubhaar, R. & Friedrich, D. (2015). Theorising and documenting the spread of Teach For All and its impact on global education reform. *Education Policy Analysis Archives. 23*(44), 1–11.

Subramanian, V. K. (2017). *Marketisation, managerialism and school reforms: A study of PPPs in elementary education in Delhi.* (Unpublished doctoral dissertation). Jawaharlal Nehru University, New Delhi.

Subramanian, V. K. (2018). From government to governance: Teach For India and new networks of reform in school education. *Contemporary Education Dialogue*, *15*(1), 1–30.

Sundar, P. (2013). *Business and community: The story of corporate social responsibility in India*. New Delhi: Sage Publications.

Teach For India. (2014). Annual report 2014–2015. Retrieved October 9, 2019 from https://www.teachforindia.org/assets/annual-report-2015.pdf

Teach For India. (2015). *Annual report 2015–2016*. Retrieved October 8, 2019 from https://www.teachforindia.org/assets/annual_report_2015_2016_low_1.pdf

Vellanki, V. (2014). Teach For India and education reform: Some preliminary reflections. *Contemporary Education Dialogue*, *11*(1), 137–147.

9. *Sign of the Times: Teach For Sweden and the Broken Swedish Education System*

P.S. Myers

Sweden

Biosketch

P.S. Myers is a Ph.D. student in the Department of Education Policy, Organization and Leadership at the University of Illinois at Urbana-Champaign. He holds an M.Ed. from DePaul University and a B.A. in African-American Studies from Northwestern University. As a traditionally-trained former teacher in public and charter schools in the Chicagoland area, his research interests include the marketization and privatization of the provision of schooling both domestically and internationally, as well as the experience of marginalized persons in these schooling arrangements.

Narrative

Since its inception, Teach For Sweden (TFS), an affiliate for Teach For All (TFAll), has received an overwhelmingly positive response in the Nordic nation idealized for its strong welfarist policy through an active branding campaign and strategic partnerships. This chapter is an attempt to see within and through the cultivated official narrative that has been offered by TFS. On its face, this chapter may not serve as a traditional counter-narrative. That is, it does not arise from an "on the ground" experience as I myself was not affiliated with TFS, but it is grounded in a rational understanding and critical analysis across a number of texts—governmental documents, news publications, organizational websites, and other promotional material.

Through this analysis, this writing fits within Peters and Lankshear's notion of a counter-narrative in that it controverts "not merely (or even necessarily) the grand narratives, but also (or instead) the official and hegemonic narratives of everyday life: those legitimating stories propagated for specific political purposes to manipulate public conspicuousness ..." (Giroux, Lankshear, McLaren, & Peters, 2013, p. 2; see also, Skolinspektionen, 2017). Writing this counter-narrative is an especially challenging endeavor as along with the other Nordic countries, Sweden is held in high regard given its international rankings of happiness as well as in the global sociopolitical imagination via its soft, normative power that exports welfarism, neutrality, environmentalism, gender parity, LGBTQIA acceptance and rights, relatively open borders for asylum seekers, along with Volvos and IKEA. With respect to Swedish education, however, something is rotten.

I became interested in Swedish education while reading scholarship around American charter schools and the movement of privatizing, market-making policy across state and national borders. Swedish *fristaende skolor* (free schools, from here forward) are an analogue to charters in that they, too, are privately managed though publicly funded. Both free schools and charters truly began to proliferate in the early 1990s. This curious, concurrent, and, as a I would later learn, connected, emergence of similar schooling ideologies and models puzzled me in my early forays into Swedish schooling. So, I understand that more often than not, when I, an American junior scholar, explain my academic interests in the Swedish pre-secondary education system to both educationalists and non-educationalists, it is meet with something between incredulity to dismissal. It is *assumed* that a nation outwardly so fair would have an educational system matching those exported, espoused, and typically upheld values. Put simply, that is not the case. Allowances can and should be made for the robust social safety net and the density of unions, though union density is on the decline overall since the early 1990s (Kjellberg, 2013) and income inequality is accelerating steeply (Pareliussen, Hermansen, André, & Causa, 2018). Still, epitomized through free schools, many of which are run for considerable profits, parents and children (i.e., students) are subjected to a highly liberalized educational apparatus (Beach, 2018) akin to a wilderness. I cast my counter-narrative from this frame: TFS is both a symbol and a harbinger of the ongoing decay within Swedish education system. The entry of TFS as an elitist actor into Swedish schooling, which is meant to "convey and anchor respect for ... fundamental democratic values that Swedish society is based on" (SFS 2010:800, Chap. 1, para. 4), affirms that this system, or at least the former democratic ideal that undergirded it, is existentially vulnerable.

This chapter proceeds with a brief history of the Swedish education system. This history is both in service to audience but also to the argument. That is, one cannot argue decay without offering evidence that past times were actually better, and the present is qualifiedly worse. From this discussion, I explain TFS's entrée and reception into the Swedish education milieu using a broad corpus of documents related to TFS's establishment. Next, I discuss the connected apparatuses and ideologies that sustain TFS. Finally, this chapter closes with a consideration of the present landscape and the possible paths forward.

A Brief History of Swedish Schooling

While the post-war history of the Swedish school system until the late 1970s was quite egalitarian, the history of the Swedish school from its beginnings up until the 1950s was marked by privatization and the influence of the church waning slowly across a century. Compulsory schooling began in Sweden in 1842 so that children could read the Bible with "their own eyes" (Florin, 2010, p. 1). The Swedish system, if that's what it could be called at that moment, was highly decentralized with "city schools for which the upper class parents paid for their children to attend, early vocational schools or schools on the estates, poor schools, parish schools, traveling schools, early childhood schools, [and] adult education" (Florin, 2010, p. 2) with stark urban and rural divides in supervision (Åstrand, 2016). The Swedish parliament began several initiatives aimed at greater standardization, centralization, and supervision during the 1850s and 1860s (Boli, 1989).

After the turn of the twentieth century and up to the 1940s, a rapidly modernizing Sweden, with improvements which reversed outward migration trends, was directed towards "a class-conscious society to a society determined by social factors, the labor movement, women's liberation, [and] democratization" (Werler & Claesson, 2007, p. 741). These changes adhered to no single set of political ideas as liberal and conservative philosophies vied with each other. Education typified this contested space, though all state-craft attempted to be rather unobtrusive (Englund, 1989), with the exception of reducing the religious influences in the state.

After World War II, a "scientific-rational" conception of education fostered a technocratic, elitist, and paternalistic Swedish state. Yet this era was possibly a golden age for the welfare state (Logue, 1979) as there was a notable reduction of poverty and increases in purchasing power across the classes. Public education also "came to be both part of the Swedish welfare state and a prominent example of it" (Forsberg & Lundgren, 2010, p. 182).

Social engineering as well as experimentation, investigation, and observation of schooling occurred in that time as educational science, though somewhat scattershot, came to the fore. Comprehensive primary school, secondary school, trade school, vocational school, adult education, and a school oversight board, Skolverket, were developed or reformed during the post-war period of Swedish school history (Werler & Claesson, 2007, p. 743). This was the Sweden that persists in the popular imagination today. The "cradle to grave," robust, albeit expensive, system of provisions whose fading is lamented by leftist and whose inefficiencies are taken as the outright failure of socialism by rightists.

Returning to the government experimentation that was in vogue during the post-war period, free schools were established. At that time, free schools, like other institutions within society during the post-war period, were sites to test social theory. Free schools could not be given public money unless they were laboratories for pedagogical and philosophical methods deemed useful by the government, a caveat that capped their expansion for roughly forty years (Olsson and Lönnström, 2011). Bunar (2008) notes that, "At the beginning of the 1980s, there were only 35 free schools, accounting for less than 0.2% of the total compulsory school student population" (p. 426).

In the early 1980s, in the idyllic western town of Drevdagen, experimentation turned into desperation as parents sought not to have their local school closed and their children bussed thirty miles away to go to school. Their plight was, and remains, reasonable. What was wrought after and through Drevdagen was a distrust of the state as a provider by employer unions as market liberalism became the cure for any failings or inefficiencies. Shortly after the Drevdagen issue was resolved with the opening of a privately-managed, publicly-funded free school, reports from a number of commissions convened by the center-right government suggested, though to varying degrees, greater flexibility within welfare provisions. One of these commissions directly warned against privatization. Yet, partnered with a predilection for free-market thinking, provisions such as eldercare, telecommunications, and schooling, were opened to private, profit-driven actors. The free school model expanded across Sweden. While there has been a steady increase in free schools in compulsory schooling, which ends at age 15, only 17% of all students attend free schools. Attendance in free school gymnasium (high school) peaked during the 2011–2012 school year with almost half of all students attending a free school (Holmström, 2018). That school year, JB Education, a Danish venture capital firm, pulled out of the free school market due to issues with profitability, leaving hundreds of families to scramble to find new schools (Orange & Adams, 2013). Still, this year roughly a third of high schoolers attend a free school with the concentration being somewhere between 40% and 60% in Stockholm (Holmström, 2018. Predictably, these private entrants shape the competitive Swedish school milieu as one not necessarily most interested in providing best chances but has opened the system to leery signals of specious value. It is within this discursive community, where public provisions remain highly critiqued, that TFS finds its entrée.

Teach For Sweden

Along with Swedish market fundamentalism and accompanying discourse, TFS's entrance was eased by a set of narratively constructed "problems" that demonstrated the legislative role in privatizing policy. The movement from "government to governance" (Geddes 2005; Jessop 2002) is reflected in Sweden's PISA crisis, shortages of qualified teachers, the degradation and denigration of teacher training, teacher blaming, and restructuring of teacher work. In short, the neoliberal Swedish establishment has forwarded a compounding set of arguments that education, namely teachers, have failed while also overseeing an educational regulatory system that hasn't been responsive to needs within the schools and classroom of Sweden. For example, though recent influxes of immigrants have exacerbated extant teacher shortages (Skolinspektionen, 2017, p. 7), shortages have existed and were predicted to worsen since the 1970s (Boucher, 1975). Additionally, the Swedish landscape of competitive, firm-like schools has forwarded a highly stressful environment where teachers are compelled to be good salespeople along with the normal day-to-day difficulties of teaching (Carlberg, 2016; Dovemark, 2017; Göransson, 2013). Though there were a number of solutions that could have been tried, the 'inventive' fix of TFS was made a centerpiece of a menu of privatized solutions in teacher preparation after 2011. The ushering of TFS into Sweden was an undertaking by a number of disparate partners bound together by their liberalizing approach. This partnership included Rektorsakademien (now called Meet in Grid) that attempts to engage school leaders in taking on practices from the world of business in order to produce entrepreneurial school leaders (Fleischer, 2015); members of the Swedish government from across a collection parties, including centrist and moderate leftist, with Mikael Damberg, a social democrat sitting on the TFS board; and one of the Swedish teachers' unions, Lärofőrbundet (Dahlström, 2013). The first mention of TFS on the floor of the Swedish Parliament is April 26, 2012 by Emil Källström of the Centrist Party (Riksdagens protokoll, 2011/12:104):

> ... If Sweden is to have a world-class schools, then the teachers are one of the more important, if not the most important, piece of puzzle. Sweden must

strengthen teachers' role and status and generally raise the attractiveness of the teaching profession. The Alliance Government has taken and takes a number of good steps in this area, but we have much left to do .... One of the problems is clearly that Swedish schools have a high proportion of unaccredited teachers. For the 2010–11 academic year, 85.9 percent of the teachers elementary schools held a pedagogical university degree. If we are to prepare the children to compete in a global market, it is not acceptable to have 14 percent of teachers are not accredited .... Today in the afternoon, some of us have attended a seminar about the Teach for America program. It may have a Swedish successor in a Teach for Sweden program where top students from our institutions after completing the degree, choose the teaching profession to make an effort and get valuable experiences. This is an example of how we can think innovatively about the provision of teachers. But because we can do that it is it is also central that the important reforms of teacher credentialization comes in place.

Källström assists in framing TFS as an elite organization using the symbolic language of the "Teach For" model by referencing the "top students" that TFS will recruit to help build "world-class schools," but also in the denigration of current schooling in Sweden. Källström ties the recruitment and retainment of Swedish teachers to notions related to human capital and market competitiveness, while ignoring many of the material realities of teachers. The seminar he referenced in the statement above featured TFA founder and TFAll co-founder and CEO, Wendy Kopp who was in Stockholm to promote the program. Video of her talk is no longer available online, but in an interview with a Swedish news program broadcast on the same day, she spoke of her "optimism" with that the "Teach For" ideology had been bought into by Läroförbundet, prospective candidates, and both the public and private sector. Indeed, regarding the private sector, Rektorsakadademien had established partnerships with a number of family-based memorial funds, but also Apple. Google AB (the branch of Google operating in Sweden) and Nordea, a Sweden-based bank, have also been long-time partners of TFS. The second mention of TFS on the official Swedish governmental record is with a budget proposal for education and research. The requested an allocation for TFS for 15,000,000 Swedish Kronor, approximately 1,655,000 USD, for the organization for its use from 2012 to 2016 (Prop. 2012/13:1). Ironically, despite critiques of the "Teach For" model supplying underprepared teachers to underprivileged classrooms being well-known at this point (Laczko-Kerr & Berliner, 2002), and with no evidentiary basis that this program would work in Sweden, this apportionment was included under "Quality-based Resource Allocation."

Similar to TFA, the TFS program of summer institute to immediate teaching while getting on-the-job pedagogical guidance from mentoring remains intact. In a slight departure while TFS focuses on university students that are not majoring in education, TFS also recruits career changers, especially from the STEM fields, into its corps. In 2012 and 2013, while TFS was taking in its first cohorts, Dagens Nyheter and Svenska Dagbladet both published editorials and opinion pieces favorably characterizing the organization that praised it for enticing top students.

From TFS's inception, I was only able to find a few critical voices (Dahlström, 2013; Samuelsson, 2013). With support extended from adult education programs and universities, print media, government officials across parties, and a number of large, multinational corporations with offices in Sweden, there seemed to be few voices willing to question either proof of the "Teach For" model or what differences the Swedish educational context might make in its delivery. This may be due, in part, to a systematic suppression of voices—a tactic that TFA has used in the United States to silence even mild criticism of their methods and results.

The TFS Narrative Echo Chamber

Since its start, TFS has only gained momentum. The organization has been insulated from critique by the overwhelmingly positive support it has received in Swedish media:

- Nine articles appeared in the Stockholm's most read newspaper, The Day's News [Dagens Nyheter], from 2012 to 2018 without substantive critique.
- Four positively framed articles appeared in more conservative Stockholm newspaper, Swedish Daily News [Svenska Dagbladet], during the same time period.
- Newspapers in Malmo, Goteborg, and Umea mostly picked up articles from the Stockholm papers, but of the originally published works, there was no attempt at critique.

Teachers unions also have positively framed TFS with 14 online articles between the two largest teacher unions since 2012 with few, if any, critiques offered. Government documents mentioning TFS appear 92 times in the official record, though some documents are redundant. Many of the documents call for funding for the program in attachment to other educational propositions—case in point, 30,000,000 Swedish Kronor, approximately 3.2 million USD, was suggested to be given to TFS in 2018 by the Education Committee of the Swedish government (Utbildningsutskottets betänkade 2017/18:UbU2). Legislators have levied little, if any, real criticism to the program, though Social Democrat, Gunila Svantorp, noted that the demands of program were "tough" in budget discussion to fund the organization (Prop.

2015/16:99). By and large, TFS and TFA, when mentioned in Swedish legislature, have been portrayed as positive routes toward teacher credentialing. Characterizing TFS as the 'next great thing' serves a raison d'etre greater than TFS: across many of the documents, the case is made for independent (i.e. free-market) actors in teacher training. With TFS as an exemplar, despite its dependence on public funding, the program can be, and is, used discursively to further additional privatizing programs at the expense of extant, and also publicly-funded, university teacher preparation programs.

TFS: The Networked Actor

Along with the aforementioned links to Google AB and Nordea, TFS builds its brand as a highly networked actor with support from a number of other private actors that commodify and enclose educational provisions. The edu-businesses and adjacent operators that are connected to TFS were well-documented by Player-Koro and Beach (2018), though, because networks are both spatial and temporal, their 2015 network map includes actors that no longer seem connected to TFS and does not include new actors that have engaged with TFS in the past three years.

An example of the former would the Swedish Postcode Lottery, which uses lottery ticket purchases to fund charitable donations. Two examples of the latter, that is, new actors, include Careerbuilder Nordic AB and Mellby Gård. Careerbuilder Nordic AB is the Swedish arm of the global job website, Careerbuilder. Though the company seemingly does not fund TFS outright, they are listed as a TFS recruiting partner that helps TFS "find more skilled leaders in the classrooms" (Teach For Sweden, 2018). In line with the Memoranda of Agreement that TFA enters with charter school operators to secure the placement of its teachers (Brewer, Kretchmar, Sondel, Ishmael, & Manfra, 2016) is TFS's agreement with Mellby Gård, parent company to Academedia, Sweden's largest free school operator (having also expanded to Germany, Norway, and elsewhere). Though TFS seemingly already had a placement relationship with Academedia, as well as 22 Swedish communes and other free school operators, the partnership and support from Melby Gård ensconced TFS as a networked member readily forwarding policies that exploit the public provision of schooling. It could be argued that TFS is not directly pushing privatizing policies, which is untrue, but partners with free school companies as a matter of survival. The question must be raised, however, if TFS's survival relies on partnering with exploitative partners, even if its goals are mostly just, then should not the organizational leadership reconsider the TFS, and inherently the entire TFAll, model? I am only left to assume that while leadership could believe in just ends, through partnering with profiteers, they have and are not fully considering the consequences of that action for all stakeholders, most especially, in this case, children.

Other People's Children

Much like its predecessors and partners, TFS ideological and pedagogical practices are operationalized out of savior narrative, based above all in deficit thinking that obfuscates complex issues, including class, ethnicity, and the failures of marketized, privatized schooling, within Swedish education. In a 2015 interpellation request to the Gustav Fridolin for funding, Sweden's education minister at this time, Moderate Maria Stockhaus (Riksdagens protokoll, 2015/16:99) explains that the fundamental idea that drives the "Teach For," and thus the TFS, model is "to make a difference for students in vulnerable areas in schools with low performance measures." TFS's website pushes the savior narrative as the simple fix to structural and allocative issues:

> Children's success in school should not be limited by their parents' education level, their school, or their socioeconomic background. We want all children to choose their own future. We believe in a world where everyone, regardless of background, has access to a comparable school .... We work for a comparable school through good leadership in classrooms based on the conviction that all children are capable.

Though the same TFS page on their site notes that parental education is a key factor in student success, their solution, to disadvantaged families in underserved areas where children experience overt and covert discriminations in who they are schooled with and, at times, depending on their ethnicity, how they are treated in schools by those peers, is the power of their brief teacher preparation program and mentorship. TFS savior narratives and deficit ideology that it (re)produces is not only a danger to students psychically (Gorski, 2011; Weiner, 2003), but it reifies stereotypes across society. In the case of Sweden, with populism and xenophobia rising, deficit models would seemingly reify nationalists' suppositions of the deleterious effect of refugees.

There is also another issue with savior narrative that is constitutive to TFS. Beyond the hubris, and even intent, the savior narrative provides cover for cynics and true-believers, alike. A logic that is disproportionately focused on teachers, whether by way of blame or reward, fails to see the role that citizens and governments have in education and does not give them impetus for change (UNESCO, 2017). While quality teaching and teachers can alter life chances for their students, the effect of "good" or "bad" teaching and teachers should not be overstated, teachers cannot be the sole course correction for Sweden's free-market failure that disadvantages the students in the marginalized and rural areas (Fjellman, Yang Hansen, & Beach, 2018).

Discussion and Conclusion

Though TFS operates quite similarly to other affiliates of TFAll, Sweden's highly liberalized education system creates a unique space for TFS. That is, TFS is not likely to be a significant provider of the nearly 130,000 full-time teacher force in Sweden any time in the near future, as their most recent cohort consisted of 61 teachers. The TFS and "Teach For" model is just as much about producing school leaders to replicate their ideology from empowered positions to increasing numbers of students. With access to and the approval of a number public and private actors that operate with less than a healthy dose of skepticism, TFS alumni will be well-positioned to affect larger numbers of students and continue to shape the narratives around what teachers can and cannot do—in all likelihood, a set of solutions that not only persists in misidentifying the problem but stands to make it worse. There is something apropos, a bit all too fitting, that there should be a TFS at all as, in many ways, it typifies the shortcomings of policy prescriptions to meet paradoxical aims—democracy through markets and equity through the gaze of elitism. Though there is room for competition and exclusivity within the negotiated space of social democracy but these conditions must be held at bay or counterbalanced by a strong notion of justice, especially for those in the margins. TFS, as an actor, network node, and ideology, is demonstrative that in today's Sweden, this balance has not been achieved.

References

Åstrand, B. (2016). From citizens into consumers: The transformation of democratic ideals into school markets in Sweden. In B. Å. Frank Adamson, Linda Darling-Hammond, London (Ed.), *Global education reform: How privatization and public investment influence education outcomes* (pp. 73–109). London: Routledge

Beach, D. (2018). Education markets and inequalities *Structural injustices in Swedish education* (pp. 235–265). Cham, Switzerland: Palgrave Macmillan.

Boli, J. (1989). *New citizens for a new society: The institutional origins of mass schooling in Sweden*. Elmsford, NY: Pergamon Press.

Boucher, L. (1975). Some aspects of teacher education and teacher supply in contemporary Sweden. *British Journal of Teacher Education*, *1*(3), 377–382. doi:10.1080/0260747750010311

Brewer, T. J., Kretchmar, K., Sondel, B., Ishmael, S., & Manfra, M. (2016). Teach For America's preferential treatment: School district contracts, hiring decisions, and employment practices. *Educational Policy Analysis Archives, 24*(15), 1–38.

Bunar, N. (2008). The free schools "riddle": Between traditional social democratic, neo-liberal and multicultural tenets. *Scandinavian Journal of Educational Research, 52*(4), 423–438. doi:10.1080/00313830802184608

Carlberg, N. (2016). Lärare som marknadsförare: En studie om hur blivande gymnasielärare ser på marknadsaspekten av sitt framtida arbete. (Dissertation, Umeå University, Umeå, Sweden). Retrieved October 19, 2019 from http://urn.kb.se/resolve?urn=urn:nbn:se:umu:diva-128395

Dahlström, L. (2013). Ni är lurade!—en kritisk granskning av Teach for Sweden. Retrieved October 1, 2019 from https://www.skolaochsamhalle.se/flode/skolpolitik/lars-dahlstrom-ni-ar-lurade-en-kritisk-granskning-av-teach-for-sweden/

Dovemark, D. (2017). Utbildning till salu–konkurrens, differentiering och varumärken. *Utbildning & demokrati, 26*(1), 67–86.

Englund, T. (1989). Educational conceptions and citizenship education. In S. Ball & S. Larsson (Eds.), *The struggle for democratic education: Equality and participation in Sweden* (pp. 32–66). New York: The Falmer Press.

Fjellman, A.-M., Yang Hansen, K., & Beach, D. (2018). School choice and implications for equity: The new political geography of the Swedish upper secondary school market. *Educational Review*, 1–22. doi:10.1080/00131911.2018.1457009

Fleischer, H. (2015). Uppdaterat: Rektorsakademien—en bisarr historia om maktfullkomlighet och ynkedom i skolsverige. Retrieved from http://www.fleischer.se/2015/06/24/rektorsakademien-en-bisarr-historia-om-maktfullkomlighet-och-ynkedom-i-skolsverige/

Florin, C. (2010). Från folkskola till grundskola 1842–1962. Retrieved from. *Lärarnas Historia*. Retrieved from http://www.lararnashistoria.se/sites/www.lararnashistoria.se/files/artiklar/Fr%C3%A5n folkskola till grundskola_0.pdf

Forsberg, E., & Lundgren, U. (2010). Sweden: A welfare state in transition. In I. Rotberg (Ed.), *Balancing change and tradition in global education reform* (Second ed., pp. 181–195). Lanham, MD: Rowman and Littlefield Education.

Geddes, M. (2005). Neoliberalism and local governance–cross-national perspectives and speculations. *Policy Studies, 26*(3–4), 359–377.

Giroux, H. A., Lankshear, C., McLaren, P., & Peters, M. (2013). *Counternarratives: Cultural studies and critical pedagogies in postmodern spaces*. New York: Routledge.

Göransson, E. (2013). Kampen om eleverna.: En undersökning om hur konkurrensen och marknadsföringen har förändrats inom gymnasieskolan. (Dissertation, Umeå University, Umeå, Sweden). Retrieved October 14, 2019 from http://urn.kb.se/resolve?urn=urn:nbn:se:umu:diva-90894

Gorski, P. (2011). Unlearning deficit ideology and the scornful gaze: Thoughts on authenticating the class discourse in education. *Counterpoints, 402*, 152–173.

Holmström, C. (2018). Friskolor i Sverige Retrieved from https://www.ekonomifakta.se/Fakta/Valfarden-i-privat-regi/Skolan-i-privat-regi/Antal-friskolor-i-Sverige/

Jessop, B. (2002). *The future of the capitalist state*. Cambridge, England: Polity Press.

Kjellberg, A. (2013). Union density and specialist/professional unions in Sweden. *Studies in Social Policy, Industrial Relations, Working Life and Mobility, Research Reports, 213*(2), 1–40.

Laczko-Kerr, I., & Berliner, D. C. (2002). The effectiveness of "Teach for America" and other under-certified teachers. *Education Policy Analysis Archives, 10*, 37.

Logue, J. (1979). The welfare state: Victim of its success. *Daedalus, 108*(4), 69–87.

Olsson, V., & Lönnström, D. (2011). *Tillsynen av fristående skolor—Rättslig och politisk förändring över tid*. Göteborg, Sweden: Sociologiska Instituionen.

Orange, R., & Adams, R. (2013). Swedish free school operator to close, leaving hundreds of pupils stranded. *The Guardian*. Retrieved from Education website: http://www.theguardian.com/education/2013/may/31/free-schools-education/

Pareliussen, J. K., Hermansen, M., André, C., & Causa, O. (2018). Income inequality in the Nordics from an OECD perspective. In J. E. Søgaard (Ed.), *Nordic Economic Policy Review* (pp. 17–57). Copenhagen: Nordic Council of Ministers.

Player-Koro, C. & Beach, D. (2017). The Influence of Private Actors on the Education of Teachers in Sweden. A Networked Ethnography Study of Education Policy Mobility. Acta Paedagogica Vilnensia, 39.

Player-Koro, C., & Beach, D. (2018). Privačių veikėjų poveikis mokytojams rengti Švedijoje. Švietimo politikos mobilumo tinklo etnografijos tyrimas. *Acta Paedagogica Vilnensia, 39*(39). doi:10.15388/ActPaed.2017.39.11476

Samuelsson, M. (2013). Lärosäten tveksamma till Teach for Sweden. Retrieved October 1, 2019 from https://universitetslararen.se/2013/04/01/larosaten-tveksamma-till-teach-for-sweden/

Skolinspektionen. (2017). *Skolan och nyanlända: En bild av Skolinspektionens senaste granskningar*. Retrieved October 1, 2019 from Stockholm: https://www.skolinspektionen.se/globalassets/0-si/08-om-oss/nyheter/sammanfattning-av-skolinspektionens-senaste-granskningar.pdf

Stochhaus, M. (2015). *Interpellation 2015/16:21* Stockholm: Sveriges Riksdag. Retrieved October 1, 2019 from https://data.riksdagen.se/fil/0F07CD7F-ACC6-4C2B-83C3-ED0693EA7AD0.

Teach For Sweden. (2018) https://teachforsweden.se.

UNESCO. (2017). *Global Education Monitoring Report: Accountabiiity in Education* Retrieved from Paris

Weiner, L. (2003). Why is classroom management so vexing to urban teachers? *Theory into Practice, 42*(4), 305–331.

Werler, T., & Claesson, S. (2007). Sweden. In W. Hörner, H. Däbert, B. Von Kopp, & W. Mitter (Eds.), *The Education Systems of Europe* (pp. 741–757): Springer Netherlands.

Swedish Laws, Propositions and Protocols

Prop. 2012/13:1. *Budgetproposition för 2013, Utgiftsområde 16, Utbildning och universitetsforskning.*
Riksdagens protokoll, 2011/12:104.
Riksdagens protokoll, 2015/16:99
SFS 2010:800. *Skollag.*
Utbildningsutskottets betänkade 2017/18:UbU2. *Utgiftsområde 15 Studiestöd.*

Index

A

Africa 3, 5, 13–23
Argentina 3, 5, 25–26, 93–97, 100, 102, 107, 109

B

Bias/Biases 125

C

Change Agent 30, 84, 86–87, 90, 120, 127
China 3, 5, 20, 39–40, 42–43, 45, 49–53, 69–71, 76–77, 80–81
Colonial 16, 30, 35, 117, 129
　Colonialism 5, 14, 56
　Colonised 34
　Colonization 23
　Decolonized 33
　Neo-Colonial 23
　Neo-Colonization 35
　Pre-Colonial 35
　Post-Colonial 33
Community 3, 26–27, 29, 31–32, 69–71, 74, 76–79, 87–88, 104–105, 111, 124–125, 139
　Communities 30–33, 35–38, 41, 51, 70–71, 74, 76–80, 94, 105, 110, 114, 125, 129

Corporate 5, 19, 23, 38, 59, 86, 119, 121–123, 127–128
Cult 62
　Cult-like 30
　"Like a cult" 62
　Cultish 62
Culture 35, 49–50, 79, 83–84, 101, 127
Curriculum 16, 20, 26, 34–35, 55, 84, 90, 94, 108, 117–118

D

Deficit
　Discourse 42–43, 50–51
　Ideologies 5
　Theorizing 30
　Thinking 48–49, 143
Dissent 36, 38, 62
　Dissenters 2, 36
　Dissenting Voices 116
Diverse/Diversity 2–3, 43–44, 71, 76, 94, 114, 117–119, 125, 128–129

E

Elite 25–26, 37, 42, 46, 57, 79–80, 140
　Elitism 5, 30–32, 37, 136–137, 144
Equality 27, 57–58, 71, 117
Experience 14, 17, 19, 34–35, 39–41, 43–48, 50–51, 56–57, 59, 70–72, 74, 76–79, 94, 97, 99–102,

104–105, 107, 109, 113, 120–122, 127–128, 135, 143
Inexperienced 56, 59

F

Failure 30, 35, 58, 60, 110, 138, 143–144
Fund 73, 141–142
   Funding 17–20, 38, 75, 86, 89, 106, 129, 141–143
   Fundraising 14

G

Global 2–4, 15–18, 20, 23, 57, 71, 83–86, 94, 96–97, 102, 109–110, 113, 119–120, 136, 140, 142

H

Hegemony 23, 31

I

Ideology 5, 23, 102, 140, 144
India 3, 5, 37, 69, 113–122, 124–130
Indigenous 30–31, 117
Inequality 5, 49, 56, 63–64, 93, 100, 110, 136
   Educational 15–16, 20, 31, 45, 57–58, 63, 71, 94, 110
Inexperience 56, 59

L

Latvia 3, 5, 83–88, 90–91
Leadership 3, 5, 15–16, 23, 29–31, 33, 36–38, 40–41, 46, 58, 64, 70–72, 77–80, 84, 87–88, 90, 94, 97–98, 100, 103, 105, 107, 113–115, 121, 123–126, 128, 135, 142–143

M

Māori 29–30, 32–35, 38, 56, 63–64
Mindlab 33, 36, 38

N

Neoliberal/ism 1, 28, 126, 128, 139
New Zealand (Aotearoa) 3, 5, 25–30, 32–38, 55–60, 63–64
North/South 14–16, 23

P

Pakeha 33–35, 38
Pasifika 56, 63–64
Pedagogy 3, 94, 98, 113, 120
Philanthropy 86
Pierre Bourdieu 40, 42–43, 46–47, 50
Poverty 21, 26, 30, 45, 55, 63, 108, 137
   Anti-poverty 49
Preparation 1, 72–73, 88–90, 139, 142–143
   of Teachers 1, 88–90, 139, 142–143
Privatization 1, 3, 135, 137–138
Privilege 14–15, 42–43, 45, 56, 98, 114, 117, 120–121, 127–129, 140

R

Race 2, 29, 34
Racism 23, 56
Recruitment 2, 39, 51, 87, 118, 140
Rural 5, 40–45, 48–51, 69–72, 76–77, 79–80, 137, 144

S

Savior
   Mentality 5
   Narrative 143
   White Savior Complex 109
Social Justice 5, 16, 31, 38, 49, 103, 115, 117
South Africa 14, 16–23

Support 16–20, 22, 28, 31, 36, 48, 60–62, 70–71, 73, 75, 79–80, 83, 86, 88–89, 100, 103, 105, 119, 125, 127–129, 141–142
Sweden 3, 5, 135–143

T

Teach For America (TFA) 1–4, 20, 23, 58, 62, 77, 79, 84, 86–88, 90, 96, 102, 114–115, 120–123, 128–129, 140–142
Testing 125, 127, 129
Training 2, 20, 33, 40–41, 45, 47–48, 50–51, 56–60, 62, 64, 71–72, 77–79, 85, 88, 90, 94, 96–100, 104, 107, 111, 116–118, 120–121, 123–124, 139, 142

U

Ubuntu 16–19, 22
Union 32, 56–57, 62, 99–100, 107, 110, 136, 138–139, 141

W

Wendy Kopp 3, 17, 77, 79, 113, 120, 140